THE SMART HOME BUYER'S HANDBOOK

About the Author

David Michael Keating, MAI, is author of two appraisal handbooks, *The Valuation of Wetlands* and *Appraising Partial Interests*, and has published several real estate articles in professional trade journals. He has been a guest speaker at national and statewide conventions of the Appraisal Institute and served on the 1994 and 1995 Young Advisory Councils held in Washington, D.C. A graduate of the real estate program at the University of Florida and a fee appraiser for 11 years, Mr. Keating currently serves as a site analyst for Winn Dixie Stores, Inc., the nation's fifth largest grocer operating in 14 states and the Bahamas. He resides in Jacksonville, Florida with his wife Amy and two children, Christopher and Carly.

THE SMART HOME BUYER'S HANDBOOK

David Michael Keating

OPEN ROAD PUBLISHING

OPEN ROAD PUBLISHING

Open Road publishes travel guides to destinations in the US and around the world, running guides, and now home guides. Write for your free catalog of all our titles.
Catalog Department, Open Road Publishing
P.O. Box 284, Cold Spring Harbor, NY 11724

1st Edition

Library of Congress Catalog Card No. 97-76012
ISBN 1-883323-72-X

TABLE OF CONTENTS

INTRODUCTION

A home provides one of the basic necessities of life – shelter. It keeps out the harsh outside elements of cold, rain, wind and snow, and provides us security and comfort. As we approach the 21st century, however, modern homes have evolved beyond just sustaining life. They influence life style.

Are you in the market for a home? If so, you're not alone. The National Association of Realtors reports nearly 4,000,000 homes are bought and sold each year. Clearly, the dream of buying and owning a home remains alive and well in America. Yet, this part of the American dream is ever more expensive and difficult to realize.

The average price of a home now exceeds $100,000 and is the typical family's greatest one-time investment. Recognizing the huge financial, social and personal costs involved, more and more shoppers are doing their homework; searching for information to make a smart home buy.

The Smart Home Buyer's Handbook was written to provide shoppers with the information needed to make a wise decision. I've learned these lessons through university study of the real estate market, more than a decade of professional work as a real estate appraiser and broker, and my own personal experience of buying, selling and leasing homes. This book will be of great assistance in making your home buying experience both enjoyable and rewarding.

OVERVIEW

The Smart Home Buyer's Handbook is a how-to book covering everything to consider when shopping for a house. The text begins with a chapter on finance and a discussion of how much home a family can afford. This chapter will acquaint readers with the world of mortgage financing and equip shoppers with the tools needed to calculate payments at various interest rate and payback schedules. This is a critical first step that will eliminate wasting time and money shopping for a house beyond one's budgetary constraints.

Chapter 2 discusses location. In real estate, location is a vital component of a successful investment and location is analyzed in terms of its linkages to important destinations. In this automobile oriented society, the most important linkages are those provided by roadway systems, such as limited access highways, primary traffic arterials and secondary feeder streets. The most important destinations to consider are the place of employment, schools, shopping, health care, and parks and how much driving time is required to access them.

Chapter 3 discusses neighborhoods. Neighborhoods are the unique subsections of town which provide a distinct set of characteristics and services to residents. Neighborhoods are analyzed in four primary aspects; economic cycle, social make-up, geographic boundaries, and government influence.

Chapter 4 discusses the homesite, which is the land supporting a home. There are three basic types of homesites; urban, suburban, and rural. Typically, urban and suburban homesites consist of lots within platted subdivisions, while rural homesites are larger and consist of tracts cut out of farms or forests. Major things to evaluate include size, shape, orientation, elevation, grade, access, utilities, zoning, and land use.

Chapter 5 discusses home design. The two most basic design types are attached and detached. Attached homes share at least one common wall with another residence while detached are stand alone structures. Important design features to consider are distinct zone placement, orientation on the homesite, friendly fronts, social backs, triangle concept kitchens, and more.

Chapter 6 discusses construction characteristics. There are myriads of combinations available in the marketplace and the fundamental types are explored. These include on-grade and off-grade foundations; exterior wall framing and veneers; roof types and covers; doors and windows; heating, ventilation and cooling (HVAC) systems; floor coverings, electrical systems, plumbing systems, security systems, etc.

Chapter 7 discusses what to consider when evaluating a used home. There are three primary types of depreciation, physical, functional, and external; with each resulting in a loss of value to the home. The information presented will enable readers to spot warning signs of depreciation and deferred maintenance, and determine which forms are curable; i.e., feasible to repair.

Chapter 8 discusses the role of brokers and whether a shopper needs one. There are four basic types of broker, with the type being a function of which party is represented. Specifically, there are buyer-brokers, seller-brokers, dual-brokers, and transaction brokers. If a broker is employed, a brokerage agreement should be executed detailing the service to be rendered, whether the employment is open or exclusive, the commission rate to be paid, and the time period involved.

Chapter 9 discusses closing the deal. Closing the deal is a three step process involving negotiations, executing a purchase and sale agreement, and consummating the transaction. This step is probably the most daunting to consumers. However, the information provided reveals the process is relatively simple, especially with the assistance of a well qualified real estate attorney.

Chapter 10 discusses what to do after the closing. Even after a house is bought, there remains work to do to transform a collection of stick, bricks and other components into home sweet home. Things to do include preparing the house for occupancy, connecting utilities, moving-in, establishing a maintenance schedule, funding a reserves for replacement account, and preparing for bumps in the road of home ownership.

Chapter 11 discusses the investment outlook for housing. The days of rapid appreciation in response to high inflation and a surge in demand from the baby boom generation appears to be over, at least for now. Therefore, the prospects of slow appreciation and the impact of the cost of leverage are explored.

Chapter 12 discusses some strategies to beat the slow forecasted appreciation within the marketplace to maximize the investment returns on your housing dollar. Strategies include buying below market value, creating value, piggybacking off the value of others, buying during the off-peak season, and avoiding the impulse buy.

The addenda contains a Summary Checklist which condenses in bullet form the main points presented. This checklist is a useful tool and reminder of important points to evaluate during the shopping process.

Enjoy.

1. HOW MUCH (HOUSE) CAN YOU AFFORD?

The first step toward smart home buying is carefully analyzing your financial position to determine how much house you can afford. By taking this first difficult step, you will eliminate wasted time and money shopping for a home beyond your means. It makes no sense (or cents) to shop diligently, negotiate aggressively, and put together a wonderful deal, only to be denied adequate financing and watch all your hard work disappear because you sought something you could not afford. For buyers which plan to pay cash for a house, your spending limits are known based on funds available in various investment accounts and this chapter can be skipped.

However, if you are like most home buyers and lack the means for an all cash transaction, then you must enter the world of mortgages and debt financing, with all its associated constraints and limitations. If this is your situation, then the information to follow will be of extreme importance.

Few buyers can afford to pay cash for a home and most must use borrowed money. The most common form of borrowed money associated with home acquisition is the mortgage. A mortgage is a pledge to repay a debt. In a home mortgage, a borrower receives funds from a lender to buy a house, and then turns around and pledges the home being acquired as collateral for repayment of the debt. The party who gives the mortgage is the mortgagor (borrower), and the party who receives the mortgage is the mortgagee (lender). Mortgages allow moderate and middle class families to buy a home they otherwise could not afford due to a lack of funds for an all cash purchase, thus providing millions of people access to an important part of the American dream.

In some states, mortgagors hold full title to the property with the mortgagee having just a lien until the debt is satisfied. These states are known as lien states. In other states, mortgagees hold title until the loan is repaid in full. These are known as title states. Obviously, borrowers prefer lien states, for the title remains in their control.

Types of Mortgages

All mortgages fall within one of four basic categories: FHA (Federal Housing Administration), VA (Department of Veterans Affairs), Conventional and Unconventional. The distinguishing feature between these types pertains to how borrower risk is underwritten. FHA and Conventional mortgages require borrowers to insure against risk of default, VA mortgages guarantee against the risk of default, and Unconventional mortgages typically have no default insurance or guarantees.

Specifically, the risk of borrower default on a debt is generally a function of the amount of the mortgage and the borrower's credit rating, income level, debts, and other such factors. Borrower default occurs when a borrower can no longer make the required loan payments. FHA and Conventional mortgage lenders require insurance to protect them against possible default if the loan amount is greater than or equal to 80% of the value of the home.

For example, if the value of a home is $120,000 and a $108,000 FHA mortgage (90% loan-to-value ratio) is being used by the buyer to acquire the home, then the lender will require the borrower to insure the amount of the loan in excess of 80%; i.e.,

$24,000. However, had the loan amount been only $95,000 (79% loan-to-value ratio), then no such insurance would be applicable. This is because lenders feel confident they can sell a home for at least 80% of its appraised value, even in a liquidation sale situation, thus recovering their investment in case of borrower default. As such, the insurance just covers the upper 20% of value.

In a VA mortgage, similar lender protections apply, but in the form of guarantees. Specifically, instead of insurance, the VA guarantees the loan amount in excess of 80%.

VA and FHA programs are government sponsored. As a result, they typically have more lenient qualifying criteria than conventional mortgages and are less costly to borrowers. However, these programs have limitations, such as limits on the value of a home which can be purchased and the type of borrowers eligible to participate. For instance, VA mortgages are only available to current or former military service personnel and can only be used once. Conventional loans are insured by third party, private mortgage insurers (PMI), and are typically more costly.

These lender underwriting criteria are important to note, for mortgage insurance and guarantees cost money. However, since few buyers can afford to put up a 20% downpayment, most are forced to participate in these insurance and guarantee programs. Your local bank and mortgage company can provide information as to current interest rates, terms and qualification requirements for these programs in your area.

Interest Rates

Unfortunately, borrowed money isn't free. It comes with a cost, and the cost of borrowed funds is known as interest. The amount of interest due is a function of the interest rate and the repayment schedule of the loan.

With mortgages, there are a variety of interest rate options available in the marketplace, but most fall within two basic categories; fixed or adjustable interest rates. A fixed interest rate means what it says - the interest rate is "fixed" and cannot be changed by the lender, even if interest rates rise. This is the least risky type of mortgage to borrowers, but the riskiest to the lender. If you plan to live in a house for a long time, or if interest rates appear to be on the rise, then a fixed rate mortgage is probably the best choice.

An adjustable rate mortgage (ARM) is just the opposite. It can change over time based on changes in interest rates. ARMs are the riskiest type of mortgage for borrowers, but the safest for lenders.

To entice borrowers to accept ARMs, banks usually charge less interest, generally a spread of 100 to 300 basis points (1% to 3%). For example, a lender may offer a fixed rate mortgage at 7.5% or a variable rate mortgage at 6%, resulting in a spread of 150 basis points. Clearly, the ARM has the more attractive interest rate, but more risk to the borrower.

Most ARM's have limits on how much the interest rate can increase (or decrease) in any given year, as well as a lifetime limit known as a "cap." Adjustments are typically tied to changes in an established index, such as changes in the yield rate of specified United States Treasury bonds. For example, an ARM may have an annual one time cap of 1% and a lifetime cap of 5%, with changes based on changes in the yields on one year Treasury notes. Therefore, if yields on short term treasuries begin to escalate, then the interest rate on the ARM can increase at a rate of up to 1% per year. However, at no time can the interest rate exceed 5% over the initial rate. Be sure to research the annual and lifetime caps of the ARMs available in your area.

Increases in the interest rate of ARMs can be devastating to your financial position unless you have adequate income. For example, every 1% increase in the interest rate of a $100,000 loan makes the payment go up $1,000 per year, or roughly $83 per month. Therefore, dealing with ARMs is risky business. If interest rates go down and stay down, you win. However, if interest rates increase rapidly, then you lose. Most people who choose an ARM believe their income will rise in the future or they plan to move or refinance in a short period of time.

Though ARMs are risky, they can be beneficial. My wife and I recently built a new house and financed our acquisition with an ARM. The interest rate we chose was 6%, while prevailing interest rates on fixed rate mortgages were 8%; a savings of 200 basis points. The ARM interest rate was fixed for 3 years, and then could adjust (up or down) at a maximum of 1% per year to a lifetime cap of 4%. In other words, the maximum interest rate possible is 10% after a 7 year worst case scenario goes as follows:

ARM INTEREST RATES	
Year	Maximum Rate
1	6%
2	6%
3	6%
4	7%
5	8%
6	9%
7	10%

As can be seen, the interest rate can go no higher than 10% due to the 4% lifetime cap. If a $100,000 mortgage is involved, the monthly payment for principle and interest based on an initial 30 year amortization schedule is as follows:

30 YEAR AMORTIZATION SCHEDULE

Year	Interest Rate	Beginning Loan Balance	Remaining Term (Yrs)	Monthly Principle and Interest Pmt
1	6.00%	$100,000	30	$600
2	6.00%	$98,772	29	$600
3	6.00%	$97,463	28	$600
4	7.00%	$96,084	27	$661
5	8.00%	$94,840	26	$723
6	9.00%	$93,707	25	$786
7	10.00%	$92,662	24	$850

As can be seen, in the worst case scenario, the loan payment could increase from $600 per month to $850 per month over seven years. This represents an increase of $250 per month, or 42%. In contrast, the monthly principle and interest payment on a $100,000 fixed rate mortgage at 8% for 30 years is $734 per month. Therefore, it will take more than 5 years with the ARM before the payment gets as high as the fixed rate mortgage, yielding interest savings of nearly $6,000. However, after five years, the payment on the ARM exceeds the payment of the fixed rate mortgage. Clearly, ARMs can be good in the short run or if interest rates remain low. The contrast is illustrated in the following graph:

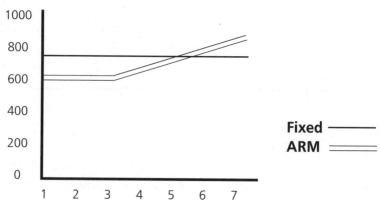

We chose the ARM because my wife is not working, but staying home to be with our young children. Since we are just a one income family, we felt the lower payment at this time was important to help maximize the use of our limited financial resources. However, in 5 to 7 years when our kids are in school, my wife plans to go back to work as a school teacher and we will be in a better position to handle the increased payment in the event interest rates should rise. Or, we can always refinance, move-up to another house, etc.

Points and Origination Fees

Most lenders charge points and origination fees. Points are up-front interest charges and only make financial sense if you plan to live in a home for a very long time. For example, for a $100,000 loan a lender may offer a 0 point, 8%, 30 year fixed rate mortgage or a 1 point, 7.75%, 30 year mortgage. The 8% interest rate yields a payment of $734 per month while the 7.75% interest rate yields a payment of $716 per month, a savings of $18 per month. Clearly, the 7.75% rate is better than the 8% rate, but a 1 point cost differential is involved. This point is applied to the loan balance and prepaid to the lender. In this case, the point equates to $1,000 (1% x $100,000). Dividing the $1,000 point charge by $18 per month yields a period of 56 months, or 4.7 years. As such, you must live in the house at least 4.7 years to make paying the point a feasible course of action. Be wary of points. They are just a way for lenders to make more money.

Also, watch out for origination fees. Most banks and mortgage brokers charge a 1% loan origination fee, equating to $1,000 on a $100,000 loan. They claim this fee is needed to process the mortgage. In reality, origination fees are often used to pay a commission to the lender's loan officer or agent. As such, be wary of origination fees.

If you shop carefully, you'll discover many credit unions and some smaller banks offer mortgage loans with no points and no origination fees. Be a wise shopper and refuse to pay points or origination fees.

Amortization Periods

Amortization periods are the time schedule over which a loan is repaid in full. They are also known as payback periods. The most common for home mortgages range from 15 to 30 years. The advantage of a shorter amortization period is the debt is paid back quicker, saving you a lot of money in interest costs. The disadvantage is the payment is higher. For example, the payment associated with a $100,000 mortgage at 8% for 30 years is $734 per month, while the same mortgage at 15 years yields a payment of $956 per month; an increase of over $200 per month. You should choose the term which best fits your financial ability, as well as your future plans and goals.

A young couple may want to go with a 30 year mortgage, for they have plenty of time to pay it off and the lower payment will enable them to afford a nicer, bigger home to support a growing family. In contrast, a couple in their early fifties may want to go with a short term note such as a 15 year mortgage, for this will allow them to pay off the loan and become debt free before retirement.

One way to enjoy the early payoff benefits of a 15 or 20 year mortgage while maintaining the lower qualifying requirements of a 30 year mortgage is to add a little extra to your housing payment each month. To do this, however, you must be sure the mortgage does not have a prepayment penalty clause. For example, in the previous example, the total payment on a $100,000 mortgage for 30 years at a fixed interest rate of 8% was $734 per month. If you added $100 per month to this payment you could pay off the mortgage in 20 years, saving 10 years worth of payments, or $88,080.

The beauty of this strategy is if times get tough and you can't make the $834 per month payment for principle and interest, your mortgage only obligates you to $734 per month. Then, when times get better, you can go back to adding $100 per month extra. The amount added and the resulting benefit varies depending on the interest rate, loan amount, and amortization period.

PAYMENT CHART

INTEREST RATE	15 Years	20 Years	30 Years
6.00%	0.0084	0.0072	0.0060
6.25%	0.0086	0.0073	0.0062
6.50%	0.0087	0.0075	0.0063
6.75%	0.0088	0.0076	0.0065
7.00%	0.0090	0.0078	0.0067
7.25%	0.0091	0.0079	0.0068
7.50%	0.0093	0.0081	0.0070
7.75%	0.0094	0.0082	0.0072
8.00%	0.0096	0.0084	0.0073
8.25%	0.0097	0.0085	0.0075
8.50%	0.0098	0.0087	0.0077
8.75%	0.01	0.0088	0.0079
9.00%	0.0101	0.009	0.008
9.25%	0.0103	0.0092	0.0082
9.50%	0.0104	0.0093	0.0084
9.75%	0.0106	0.0095	0.0086
10.00%	0.0107	0.0097	0.0088
10.25%	0.0109	0.0098	0.009
10.50%	0.0111	0.01	0.0091
10.75%	0.0112	0.0102	0.0093
11.00%	0.0114	0.0103	0.0095
11.25%	0.0115	0.0105	0.0097
11.50%	0.0117	0.0107	0.0099
11.75%	0.0118	0.0108	0.0101
12.00%	0.012	0.011	0.0103

Payment Chart

The previous chart will help you estimate the applicable monthly mortgage payment based on interest rates ranging from 6% to 12% and terms of 15, 20 and 30 years. You can calculate the appropriate monthly payment by multiplying the loan amount you will be borrowing (typically 80% to 97% of the purchase price) by the factor in the chart. This chart only applies to fixed rate mortgages, for payments associated with adjustable rate mortgages can vary over time.

For example, assume you want to borrow $120,000 to buy a $140,000 home, and the terms of your mortgage include a 7% interest rate and a 30 year amortization period. The factor in the chart above for 7% and 30 years is 0.0067. Multiplying this factor by $120,000 equates to a payment of $804 per month for principle and interest payments. Likewise, if the interest rate is 8% and a 15 year term is involved, the factor is 0.0096. Multiplying this factor by $120,000 equates to a payment of $1,152 per month for principle and interest payments.

Real Estate Taxes and Insurance

To estimate the total applicable housing payment, insurance and real estate taxes must also be included. Property insurance protects you and the mortgage company from potential loss in the value of your home which may result from a fire, storm, flood or other disaster. Call at least three insurance companies to get a good estimate of this cost, and don't necessarily go with the cheapest policy. Be sure the company you choose has a good credit rating, as well as a good history of handling claims.

To estimate real estate taxes, call the local government property appraiser. If the home is more than a year old it will most likely be on the tax rolls, and assessor personnel can inform you of the actual amount of taxes charged. If the home is new, then talk to one of the field appraisers as to the typical assessed taxes of homes in the area.

Sources of Mortgages

There are many sources of mortgage funds. By far, the largest source of FHA, VA, and Conventional home mortgages are banks and credit unions. Savings and Loan (S&L) institutions were formerly the largest mortgage originator, but fell from grace during the late 1980s; costing taxpayers billions of dollars in an expensive bailout of the industry. In general, credit unions are less expensive and offer better terms than banks. This is because credit unions are typically not-for-profit institutions owned by members. In contrast, banks are for-profit institutions and due to a recent wave of acquisitions and mergers, there are fewer banks resulting in less competition and higher fees to consumers.

Another source of mortgage funds is a mortgage broker. Such a broker sells mortgages and acts as an agent for banks, pension funds, insurance companies, real estate investment trusts (REITs), and others interested in investing dollars in home mortgages. Such a broker can help you shop for a good interest rate and term, but his services involve a fee. Therefore, you probably can save a couple thousand dollars doing your own homework and financing with a credit union or small consumer friendly bank. However, for those without much time or care, a mortgage broker provides a helpful service.

(Pre)Qualifying

After determining which type of mortgage program, interest rate and amortization schedule is best for you, then its time to prequalify. Prequalifying is an informal, nonbinding assessment of your potential borrowing strength. This is a very important step, for it will help determine how much home you can afford. It begins by making an appointment with the lender offering the best interest rate and no point - no origination fee mortgage in the area.

When meeting with the lender for a pre-qualification analysis, the loan officer will ask questions pertaining to your financial position, especially concerning your income, job history, debts, bank account balances, and other such information. Be truthful in answering all such questions. Making false statements on a mortgage application is fraud, a potential felony act punishable by imprisonment and fines.

After answering all the questions and filling out the appropriate forms, the lending officer will typically perform a series of calculations based on type of loan, interest rates, terms and other criteria involved. Then, he will provide you with the home price and monthly payment you can afford under the relevant mortgage underwriting guidelines. With this information in hand, you can begin to search for a home within the parameters of what you can afford.

There are two important ratios that lenders consider when determining your borrowing ability. These are the housing expense ratio (HER) and the total obligations ratio (TOR).

The housing expense ratio is monthly housing expenses divided by monthly gross income, while the total obligations ratio equates to the housing expense ratio adjusted for other obligations such as car payments, boat payments, and other credit payments. For example, if a mortgage will result in a housing expense of $700 per month for principle, interest, taxes and insurance (PITI), and the borrower earns a gross monthly income of $2,400 per month, then the resulting housing expense ratio equate to 29% as follows:

$$HER = \frac{\text{Housing Expense}}{\text{Monthly Gross Income}}$$

Inserting numbers yields:

$$HER = \frac{\$700}{\$2,400} = 29\%$$

If the borrower also had a $300 per month car payment and a $200 per month boat payment, then total monthly obligations would be $1,200 per month ($700 house + $300 car + $200 boat = $1,200). As such, the total obligations ratio would be 50% as follows:

$$TOR = \frac{\$700 + \$300 + \$200}{\$2,400}$$

$$= \frac{\$1,200}{\$2,400}$$

$$= 50\%$$

For FHA mortgages, the housing expense ratio generally cannot exceed 29%, and the total obligations ratio generally cannot exceed 41%. For conventional mortgages, the housing expense ratio typically ranges from 25% to 28% and the total obligations ratio ranges from 33% to 38%. The effect of these lower ratios associated with conventional mortgages makes it harder to qualify.

For example, if we consider the same $700 a month payment for PITI on a home and a 25% conventional loan housing ratio, then the amount a borrower must earn to qualify is $2,800 per month ($700 ÷ 25%), or $33,600 per year. However, under the 29% FHA housing expense ratio, the borrower would only need to earn $2,400 per month ($700 ÷ 29%) or $28,800. There-fore, the lower ratio means a borrower must earn roughly $4,800 per year more than if the borrower had qualified under the FHA ratio. As can be seen, the government programs were devel-oped to assist home buyers.

Recourse in Case of Default

It is important to recognize the implications of a mortgage. If a borrower defaults and quits making payments before a loan is repaid in full, then the lender can evict him from the house, toss all his furnishings into the street, sell the house to repay all in-debtedness, and drag the borrower into court seeking addi-tional funds if the sale of the home did not fully satisfy the debt and accrued legal fees. It doesn't matter if the borrower could no longer make payments due to job loss, sickness, disability, death or other legitimate crisis. Laws protect mortgagees.

When you give a mortgage, you become an indentured servant of sorts; promising to work hard and pay back the loan. As a result, you are not free from the lender's yoke until the loan in paid back in full.

In cases of borrower default, lenders generally have two poten-tial courses of action, with recourse dependent on the type of loan involved. In the case of a "nonrecourse" mortgage, the home is the sole collateral. As such, if the borrower defaults, the lender can seize the home and sell it to recover the debt owed and accrued legal fees. However, the sole source of re-course becomes the price of the house in a liquidation sale. No other assets or income of the borrower can be claimed.

In a "recourse" mortgage, the lender can claim the house and hold the borrower personally liable for any residual debt and legal fees. In such cases, if the sale of the home does not gener-ate funds sufficient to pay off the outstanding mortgage debt, then the lender can lay claim to other cash and assets owned by the borrower, such as income or some types of savings accounts. Be it known, a mortgage is serious business.

Common Terminology

When you enter the realm of mortgages, the terminology may be foreign. Lenders have certain terms they use, which can become confusing to consumers. To assist you in understanding the lingo, the following is a glossary of some common home finance terms:

Mortgage: a pledge to repay a debt involving real estate as collateral.

Mortgagor: the party which gives the pledge; borrower.

Mortgagee: the party which receives the pledge; lender.

Interest Rate: the cost of borrowed funds.

Fixed Rate Mortgage: mortgage involving a fixed interest rate, which cannot change.

Adjustable Rate Mortgage (ARM): mortgage involving a floating, variable interest rate. Typically, changes are linked to the movement of a specified index and are limited to an amount per year. Most include a lifetime cap.

Points: interest charges paid up-front, generally to buy-down the interest rate.

Amortization Period: the period required to payback the loan in full.

Fully Amortizing Loan: the entire principle with interest is paid back over the term of the loan.

Partially Amortizing Loan: only part of the principle along with associated interest is paid back over the term of the loan. This type includes a balloon, which is a large amount due at the end of the loan term.

Interest Only Loan: only interest is paid and all of the principle (loan amount) is due at the end of the loan term.

Conventional Mortgage: a mortgage originated with a bank or other financial institution in which no government mortgage insurance or guarantees apply.

Unconventional Mortgage: a mortgage originated with a party other than a financial institution, such as a loan from a friend or family member and seller held financing.

Federal Housing Administration (FHA): government agency involved with many housing oriented programs, including mortgage insurance for home buyers.

Veterans Administration (VA): government agency involved with veteran's affairs. Offers special mortgage guarantee program for veterans of the U.S. armed forces.

Private Mortgage Insurance (PMI): insurance which protects conventional mortgage lenders from default losses associated with loan-to-value ratios greater than 80%, paid by the borrower.

Equity: home value less outstanding debt. At acquisition, equity is often reflected by the amount of downpayment applied.

Loan-to-Value Ratio (LTV): the loan amount divided by the value of the house. Calculated as follows:

$$LTV = \frac{\text{Loan Amount}}{\text{House Value}}$$

Equity-to-Value Ratio (ETV): the equity amount divided by the house value. Also can be calculated as follows:

$$ETV = 1 - LTV$$

Housing Expense Ratio (HER): monthly housing expenses divided by monthly gross income.

$$HER = \frac{\text{Monthly Housing Expenses}}{\text{Monthly Gross Income}}$$

Total Obligations Ratio (TOR): housing expense ratio adjusted for other obligations.

$$TOR = \frac{\text{Housing Expenses + Other Obligations}}{\text{Monthly Gross Income}}$$

Summary

In summary, most home buyers cannot pay cash for a house and must use a mortgage loan. This type of loan is typically collateralized by the house, as well as other personal assets of the borrower. There are four basic types of mortgages; FHA, VA, Conventional and Unconventional. The main difference between them pertains to how the mortgage risk is underwritten. A buyer's ability to qualify for a mortgage is a function of several factors such as credit history, income, other obligations, and the amount of the house payment. If you are in healthy financial shape, then you can prequalify yourself to estimate how much house you can afford. A table with interest rates and loan terms was provided to assist you in this endeavor.

Now that you know how much house you can afford, its time to start shopping. The following chapters provide information to evaluate and consider during the shopping process.

2. LOCATION, LOCATION, LOCATION

Location! Location! Location! This buzz phrase is common lingo in real estate circles and its importance cannot be overemphasized. Location is critical to satisfaction. Buying the right house in the wrong location is never the right choice.

Granted, people don't always have the opportunity to live in the location of their dreams. Our choices are limited by factors such as job availability, income, tolerance of different climates, the desire to be near (or away from) family members, dream retirement area, and other such factors. Therefore, a discussion of the pros and cons of living in one area of the country versus another, such as the coast versus the heartland, is not within the scope of this chapter. Rather, the factors to consider when analyzing various locations within the particular city or region where you have chosen to live will be explored.

Location is a function of linkages to other properties, and linkages are the time and distance relationships between one property and another. With respect to housing, the most important linkages are those provided by roadway and mass transit systems. Specifically, a roadway or mass transit system providing quick and convenient access to the place of employment is a good locational feature. In contrast, a lack of good linkages to work is a poor locational feature. Thus, our discussion of location begins with a discussion of linkages.

Roadway Systems

Roadways are the most important linkage because we live in an automobile oriented society. This reliance on self-transportation is partly a result of America's character of independence and avoidance of relying on others, as well as the suburban sprawl which has created a great divide between the places where people live and the places where people work.

As a result, most people use an automobile to access the workplace, the shopping center, the doctor's office, and other destinations. In the future, this may change as more and more metropolitan areas strive to develop mass transit systems in an attempt to lessen traffic congestion, pollution, and other problems associated with overcrowded roadways. However, if mass transit is not available, then pay close attention to the quality of roadway systems in an area.

A well located home will be served by the following types of roads:

1) Secondary feeder streets

2) Primary traffic arterials

3) Limited access highways

Secondary feeder streets are the smallest of the three and typically consist of two lane facilities traversing through residential and rural areas. Such roadways generally serve to provide access to housing and "secondary" uses such as schools, churches and parks. Because of the residential, agricultural and institutional nature of development along these streets, they are often speed restricted from 25 to 35 miles per hour. In addition, they generally have stop signs as opposed to traffic lights, for traffic along these roadways is generally not very congested.

Below is a picture of a secondary feeder street.

Secondary Feeder Street

Primary traffic arterials are wider than secondary feeder streets and are built to service a greater volume of traffic. Most have three to six lanes and link with commercial destinations such as shopping centers, office buildings, restaurants, and medical facilities. The speed limit on these roadways typically ranges from 40 to 55 miles per hour and include busy intersections improved with traffic lights. In highly developed areas, primary traffic arterials can become congested during peak use (rush) hours resulting in bumper-to-bumper conditions.

Below is a picture of a primary traffic arterial.

Primary Traffic Arterial

Limited access highways are the third type of roadway and typically consist of divided expressways with four or more lanes of traffic such as are found in the interstate highway system and many toll expressways. As the name implies, these roadways have limited access, which means you can only get on and off at certain points, called interchanges. Many limited access highways contain a grassy median to separate opposing lanes of traffic. Speed limits typically range from 55 to 75 miles per hour and they do not have any stop lights to slow traffic.

Below is a picture of a limited access highway.

Limited Access Highway

In general, it is wise to seek a home which has good linkages via all three roadways mentioned. In particular, it is wise to live along a small, lightly traveled, narrow secondary feeder street which provides convenient, short links to schools and parks. Such a street should be curved to slow traffic and include street lighting (though not overly bright). Tree lined streets are a benefit. Trees enhance the appeal of an area and also serve as a natural barrier, protecting property from cars and other vehicles along the street. These locational criteria help to minimize speeding traffic and maximize the safety of children and pets. In addition, such a location minimizes noise, pollution, and crime.

It is also wise to live near, but never along, primary traffic arterials providing quick and easy access to places of employment, shopping centers and health care facilities. It is important these traffic arterials flow efficiently without excess congestion, even during rush hours (a rare find these days). Such a roadway should include access via a traffic light, so you aren't stuck waiting for a break in traffic to get on and off the arterial.

Lastly, it is convenient to locate within reasonable proximity to an interstate highway, particularly if such a highway is the best linkage to work or if you travel often to other areas of a region and state.

A good example of an efficient road network containing secondary feeder streets, primary traffic arterials, and limited access highways is our blood circulation system. The small blood vessels which feed the muscles and tissues in our arms and legs are like secondary feeder streets. They can't handle much blood flow (traffic) and don't go very far (cul-de-sacs and dead end streets). These blood vessels flow into larger veins in the arms and legs which serve as primary traffic arterials. Veins handle a much greater flow of blood; passing through vital organs (shopping center, places of employment, and health care facilities) and connecting with major arteries. Arteries provide direct access to the heart and are designed to carry a high volume of blood. They are like limited access highways, for access is only found in certain spots.

A healthy body needs an efficient blood circulation system. If veins and arteries become filled with cholesterol, fatty buildup, or other restrictions, then blood doesn't flow properly and a person's health suffers. Likewise, in roadway systems, if secondary streets and primary traffic arterials are not adequately designed or are congested, then bumper-to-bumper traffic can result. This causes time delays, longer commutes to work, increased stress levels and other undesirable effects which have a negative effect on your life. Thus, it is important to locate in an area which provides an efficient flowing roadway system with plenty of capacity to facilitate additional development.

The best way to test the health of a roadway system is to get out and drive during peak (rush) hours, which normally range from 7:00 a.m. to 9:00 a.m. and from 4:00 p.m. to 6:00 p.m., Monday through Friday. If you can get around easily and timely during these hours, then it will be even easier during off peak hours. Repeat the commute for several days to make sure you didn't test the route on a particularly good or bad traffic day. A forty minute drive along a swift moving freeway is tolerable, but a forty minute drive in bumper-to-bumper, stop-and-go traffic with a traffic light at every corner can be nerve wracking.

Don't gamble on the outer edge of your tolerance level, for the roadway to work will most likely get worse, not better, in the future, and you may find the time and aggravation factors escalating beyond your sanity threshold. This is important to consider since psychologists are discovering the stresses associated with slow moving commutes can have serious effects on a person's physical and mental health over time.

Another means of determining congestion levels is to analyze the trend in traffic counts. Traffic count statistics can usually be obtained free of charge from local government and state road departments. These counts show the number of automobiles using a roadway over time. If counts are escalating at a rapid pace, then the current ease of travel afforded by a roadway may soon deteriorate. Also, talk to road department personnel about capital improvements such as road widening projects or new roads which are planned to keep traffic flowing efficiently. Road department personnel know such plans five and ten years in advance and will be able to provide the needed information.

Mass Transit Systems

In some places, mass transportation systems are present. Mass transit can be a popular, economical, and practical alternative to driving, and in the future more and more people may choose to leave their automobile in the garage and ride such systems.

Types generally include subways, trains, trollies and busses. If these are available in your area, then evaluate costs and benefits. Costs include riding fees and the loss of freedom associated with not having access to your automobile during the day. Benefits may include the savings associated with only needing one car for the family and riding time can be spent productively, such as in working or reading a good book. If benefits exceed costs, then consider a location near a terminal.

Destination: Work

One of the most important destinations which should be considered is the place of employment. A full time working person generally makes more trips to their place of employment than trips to any other destination. For example, trips to work generally exceed trips to school, trips to shopping centers, trips to the doctor, trips to church, etc. Therefore, locating near work can significantly impact a person's lifestyle and supply of leisure time.

Every area generally has employment hubs for various types of industries. For instance, those employed in white collar industries such as banking, accounting, and law are often housed in office buildings located in a downtown area near the local seat of government, or in a suburban office campus setting. Similarly, those employed in blue collar industries such as manufacturing, warehousing and wholesaling are often located in industrial hubs near railroads, airports, seaports and other places where raw materials and finished goods have access to good shipping facilities.

When evaluating links to work; avoid living west of your place of employment if possible. Such a location means you will drive into the glare of the sun in the morning on your way to work, and then drive into the glare of the sun in the afternoon on your way home. I did this for many years and it was not only aggravating, but dangerous.

Destination: Schools and Parks

If you have children, then the quality and proximity of schools and parks is a high priority locational consideration. Unfortunately, not all schools are of comparable quality. There are good ones and bad ones. If possible, parents will seek to remove their children from poor quality school districts and flee to good quality districts. It has been my experience that parents are willing to double or triple their commute time to work and live in a far removed suburb if that's what it takes to ensure their child has access to good schools. But what constitutes a good school? Basically, academic performance, quality and training of staff, quality and condition of facilities, and funding for programs.

The first place to start in evaluating the quality of schools in an area is to ask long time residents who have raised kids in the community. Such residents may be co-workers at the place of employment, fellow worshipers at church or synagogue, or friends at the golf club, tennis club, or other social venue. They will typically know the good and bad districts and provide basic general information and trends.

While the opinions of others is a good place to start, decisions must be made on cold, hard facts. Therefore, the next step in researching schools is to request a list of test results from district or state educational administration agencies. These results should include the test performance of students at each school in comparison to the performance of students at other schools in the district and state. From this data, it is relatively easy to determine which schools are achieving the highest academic performance.

While historic data and trend analysis is useful, it is not always indicative of future performance. Therefore, examine the qualifications of the existing teaching and administrative staff, especially those in the grades which your child will be attending. At a minimum, teachers should be well trained and have a four year bachelor's degree in education corresponding with the grade level in which they instruct (i.e., elementary, secondary, special needs or gifted). In addition, teachers should be state certified; an indication they have passed a competency test. Ideally, the teacher should have at least a few years of experience with a student passing percentage in line or exceeding that of other teachers in the area. Most public schools have standard minimum qualifications for their staff, but the requirements of private schools vary widely.

Research information pertaining to the student teacher ratio. Most public schools have a higher student teacher ratio than private schools, primarily due to funding restrictions. It is not uncommon for public schools to have a student-to-teacher ratio of 25:1 to 35:1, while private schools may afford a lower ratio of 15:1 to 20:1. Many school officials downplay the effect of a high student-to-teacher ratio, but don't believe them. More students in a classroom means less individual time per student and more chances of getting a disruptive "bad apple."

Examine funding levels for the district and individual school you are investigating. Funding levels should be stable-to-increasing. Cuts in funding are indicative of serious financial and administrative problems, such as an eroding tax base or declining enrollment. Also, examine the quality and condition of facilities. Typically, public schools are well built and maintained, but this is not always the case with private schools. Again, signs of poor maintenance are an indication of financial or management problems. Note: the buildings don't have to be brand new, but they should be well kept.

Lastly, examine the strategic plan of the school district, including plans for new schools, technology and programs. Try to find out if too much funding is being allocated to facilities as opposed to programs, equipment and teachers. The most important things are not new buildings, but good academic performance, interesting programs of study, the availability of computer technology for student use, and a low student-to-teacher ratio. I think you'll also find that every school district has a favorite son; i.e., a school which somehow receives more money for the things it needs. Such schools are the "shining examples" of the district. Seek to locate near such a school.

Parks are important to adults as well as children. Many studies are now indicating that people want to live near and within walking distance of open green space areas such as are found in a park setting. Features to look for include large open areas with well kept grass and landscaping; playground equipment anchored to the earth, free of exposed bolts, screws or other sharp objects; as well as facilities such as a volleyball court, tennis court, basketball court and fields for baseball or soccer. Well maintained restrooms are also beneficial. A nearby park can provide a safe attraction for kids and families.

Destination: Shopping Centers

Shopping centers are an important destination, for they are the place families frequent to buy food, medicine, clothing and sundry items. Basically, shopping centers can be grouped within three classes; neighborhood centers, community centers, and regional centers.

The neighborhood shopping center is the smallest of the three and generally ranges in size from 30,000 to 100,000 square feet. They house tenants such as grocery stores, drug stores, hair salons and ice cream shops. You will most likely frequent them on a weekly basis to purchase food, drugs and sundry items. To facilitate access, they are usually developed on corner sites near subdivisions, apartment or condominium complexes, and other places of housing development.

The community shopping center is bigger than the neighborhood shopping center and typically ranges in size from 100,000 to 300,000 square feet. These centers often house a discount store such as Target, Wal-Mart or K-Mart, and a bigger variety of local specialty stores such as a pet store, golf shop and restaurant. Community shopping centers are usually accessed a few times a month, but not as much as neighborhood centers. They are typically found along primary traffic arterials, often at busy intersections improved with traffic lights.

The last type of shopping center is the regional mall which consists of the enclosed mall or discount outlet mall. In areas with a population of several hundred thousand people there may be only one such center, whereas in areas with millions of people there may be several. The most typical form of regional shopping center is the enclosed mall which houses tenants such as department stores, jewelry stores, movie theaters, restaurants and others. Malls typically contain over 300,000 square feet, with most containing at least one million square feet. Linkages to these centers are not as important, since mall shopping is only done periodically or on weekends when convenience is not as much a concern.

Destination: Medical Care

Another important destination to consider is that of proximity to health care facilities. Fortunately, most areas have a good supply of doctors, dentists, and veterinarians. Therefore, the main health care destinations I would like to bring to your attention are those of emergency and extended care facilities.

Most areas now have three sources of emergency care, the traditional hospital emergency room, the relatively new concept of suburban primary care centers, and the local fire/rescue station.

The most comprehensive emergency care is generally found in hospitals. They are the best equipped to handle a wide variety of emergencies and are convenient if subsequent admittance for extended care is required. However, hospitals are regional facilities and may not be near attractive places to live.

Primary care centers, also known as "doc in the box" facilities, are typically designed to handle minor emergencies such as broken bones, lacerations requiring stitches, and sicknesses during odd hours. They generally offer services at a much reduced cost as compared with hospital emergency rooms. These facilities are becoming popular and are sprouting up in suburban locations convenient to housing nodes.

Fire/rescue teams are the last form of emergency care. They can provide quick on-site assistance, but will generally transport victims to hospitals for complete evaluation and treatment. Do some research and discover whether nearby fire/rescue stations are staffed by paramedics and emergency medical technicians (EMTs). Also, call and ask the typical response time of squads in your area. Generally, an emergency call to a fire/rescue squad is the result of a life threatening situation.

If you live in an area served by several hospitals, identify the hospital with the best reputation and most up-to-date equipment, and make sure your doctors practice out of that hospital. Most doctors are linked to particular hospitals, and if you're not careful they may not practice at the hospital of your choice. Therefore, do your homework before you or a family member gets sick and identify the best hospital and doctors in the area. Then, God forbid a crisis emerge, you'll be ready and can avoid changing hospitals and doctors while ill.

Attractions and Nuisances

In addition to important destinations, linkages to area attractions and nuisances should be evaluated, for such linkages directly affect the value and desirability of a specific location. Examples of attractions include scenic lakes, rivers, oceans, mountains, and valleys. Such beautiful natural landscapes enhance the aesthetic and recreational features of a location, and thus increase its value. Every town offers some form of attraction, so try to be as close to it as your budget will allow.

In contrast, nuisances have a negative impact on values. Nuisances include airports, landfills (garbage dumps), power generating stations, gasoline bulk storage facilities, chemical plants, military bases, and large industrial/manufacturing complexes. Such places emit noises, pollution, and pose dangers associated with explosions, disasters, and other causes of property damage and personal injury. Avoid living near a nuisance, for these have a negative impact on values.

Summary

In summary, we can't always live where we want, but we can make wise housing choices where we live. Every potential home buyer should carefully consider location. A well located home generally fronts a secondary feeder street, has quick access to primary traffic arterials and limited access highways, and also enjoys good linkages with important destinations such as places of employment, schools, parks, shopping centers, and medical care facilities. Lastly, a well located home is nestled near value enhancing attractions, and far removed from dangerous nuisances.

3. NEIGHBORHOODS

If a city or town can be likened to a pizza, then neighborhoods are the slices. Potential home buyers should find the neighborhood which satisfies their tastes and desires, and pick that slice of town as the location for their home. Specifically, a neighborhood is a subsection of a larger overall area which shares a common character and contains the needed social services and facilities to adequately support residential development. The common character aspects of neighborhoods are associated with the real estate term "conformity." A healthy neighborhood has conforming land uses, whereas a sick or declining neighborhood doesn't.

For example, a stable or growing neighborhood will usually contain a large percentage of single family homes in good, well kept condition, situated within subdivisions improved with sidewalks, playgrounds and landscaped entrances. There will be good quality shopping centers nearby containing grocery and drug stores, and maybe even a nearby regional shopping mall. There will be office buildings where residents can work, plenty of medical care facilities, and a hospital within a short drive. There will also be good quality schools, parks, and other public works sponsored by the relatively affluent tax base. This type of neighborhood generally yields the best prospects for long term appreciation.

In contrast, a declining neighborhood may contain old housing which lacks proper maintenance. Often, there is industrial encroachment; i.e. the presence of warehouses and factories spilling into residential areas. The neighborhood will typically enjoy nearby shopping centers, but the stores will be older, less well maintained, and more discount oriented. This type of neighborhood is not necessarily inferior, but usually yields lower home values and more unstable prospects for appreciation.

Granted, the examples presented are stereotypes and should be taken in context. However, most people have passed through similar areas and can relate to them. The key to a successful home purchase is to find the neighborhood which best meets your needs, desires, and budgetary constraints.

Before diving too deep into this subject, I want to strongly emphasize that the best neighborhood is not necessarily the newest or most affluent, and race/ethnic orientation should never be a consideration. For example, a two bedroom 1,400 square foot home on a golf course in an affluent neighborhood may sell for over $200,000. However, that same $200,000 may buy a five bedroom 3,000 square foot home in a good quality middle-class neighborhood in the suburbs. Therefore, buying a home in the most affluent section of town generally means paying a premium for intangible elements such as status. Such intangibles may not be as important to you as home size, number of bedrooms, and proximity to schools.

There are four primary forces you should consider when evaluating neighborhoods. These include economic, social, geographic, and governmental forces.

Economic Forces

Neighborhoods transition between four economic cycles over time. These life cycles include growth, maturity, decline, and revitalization. It is a wavelike cycle illustrated by the following exhibit:

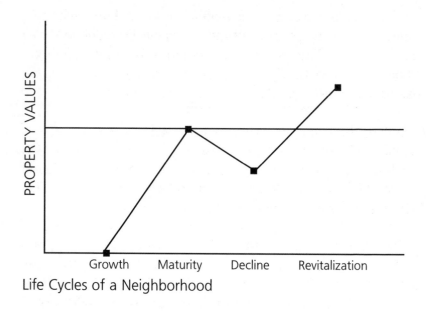

Life Cycles of a Neighborhood

The first stage in the cycle is growth. This stage occurs as population and demand for housing in an area increase to the point that raw land is purchased by developers and subsequently converted into housing. Shopping centers, office buildings, schools and other support facilities are then developed to serve the growing population. The growth cycle continues in a neighborhood until demand subsides and/or there is little land remaining to support additional development. Depending on the boundaries of a neighborhood, the growth cycle typically ranges from 20 to 30 years, afterwhich development moves on to "newer" neighborhoods which have more land available.

The maturity stage follows. Demand remains strong for housing during this cycle, but most of this demand is satisfied by the resale of existing homes and the slow development of new homes on scattered undeveloped interior parcels. This stage often lasts approximately 10 to 20 years.

The decline stage follows the maturity stage. It usually sets in when the housing stock begins to reach the age of roughly 50 to 60 years. At this age, buildings are typically in need of renovations or are becoming physically compromised and functionally obsolete. Declining neighborhoods typically pose the greatest risk to investors. As such, I don't recommend buying a home in declining areas unless you feel very confident that revitalization is rapidly approaching.

The last stage is revitalization. This stage may take a very long time to begin once decline has set in. In revitalization, people renovate and upgrade old, outdated homes, to current standards. In general, this stage only occurs in areas which offer a special feature which is valued and in short supply in a region, such as water frontage, mountain views, proximity to downtown, historically significant architecture, etc. Investing in this stage of the economic cycle often holds the greatest potential for investment return and profit. However, it is also very risky. I typically don't recommend buying a home in a revitalizing neighborhood if you have children, or if you can't afford to risk losing part of your investment. I will discuss investing in revitalizing neighborhoods in a later section of this book.

The cycle which offers the safest investment prospects with good potential for appreciation is the growth stage. The cycle which poses the greatest risk of loss in value and should generally be avoided is the declining stage. Overall, the maturity cycle offers stability, except as it approaches decline, and the revitalization cycle holds the greatest potential for appreciation and return on investment, but is very risky.

Besides analyzing the life cycles of neighborhoods, another economic consideration to research is the proportion of the housing stock which is owned versus the proportion which is rented. If you are buying a home, then concentrate on areas where the vast majority of the housing stock is owner occupied. This protects your value, for, unfortunately, renters are more transient and don't take care of property as well as owners. Therefore, if there are a lot of rental homes in the neighborhood, then the condition of housing may begin to decline along with the quality and stability of your neighbors. The best way to determine the proportion of owners versus renters is to reference the U.S. Census. In addition, the census reports average home values, average family income levels, the average age of the housing stock, and other socioeconomic data.

Social Forces

Economics teaches us the interaction of supply and demand determines price. If demand for a product increases while supply is held constant, then price will increase. In contrast, if demand for a product decreases while supply is held constant, then price will decrease. Most economists concur the real estate supply curve is relatively constant in the short run, for it typically takes 3 to 6 months to build a house. Therefore, if the population in an area is growing (demand is increasing) and the housing supply is relatively constant, then house prices will tend to increase. This is the basis of appreciation.

To position yourself to enjoy increased wealth through property appreciation, it is important to buy a home in a growing area or in an area predicted to experience such growth in the near future. Reciprocally, avoid buying a home in an area with a stagnant or declining population, for such trends will erode the value of your investment over time.

A good source of population trend information is the local city or county planning department. These usually have current census count information for neighborhoods, as well as future projections. Accessing this information is typically free of charge and can be of great assistance in evaluating demand trends. An example of what to look for in population information is provided below. This information pertains to population growth within a popular neighborhood of Jacksonville, Florida:

Population Growth			
	1970	**1980**	**1990**
Population	3,399	9,864	26,077
10 Yr. Increase		6,465	16,213
% Increase		290%	264%

As can be seen, the population within the neighborhood nearly tripled from 1970 to 1980, and increased by over 250% from 1980 to 1990. These trends indicate a very rapid rate of population growth. As a result, home prices have been escalating. Therefore, a growing population is good for housing values.

Median age is another important social factor to consider. In general, people are happier living amongst their peers and this is evident based on trends. For example, singles and newly married couples tend to live in apartment complexes and starter home developments where the majority of other residents are singles and newly married couples. Families with children tend to live in neighborhoods filled with other children, playgrounds, sidewalks, and in close proximity to good schools. Empty nesters and retirees tend to down scale their housing needs and purchase smaller homes and condominiums which offer less maintenance and more social interaction. Buying right in this manner can significantly impact the quality of your desired lifestyle.

Geographic Forces
Neighborhoods are delineated by natural and man-made boundaries. Natural boundaries include rivers, lakes, mountains, valleys, oceans and similar geographic formations, and man-made boundaries include roads, bridges, dams, reservoirs, fence lines, and other such man-made improvements. Both serve as buffers to continuous development.

Before buying a home, carefully investigate the geographic features of a neighborhood. In general, it is better to live in an area with favorable land characteristics and abundant natural resources than in neighborhoods lacking such. Neighborhoods containing lakes, rivers, streams, mountains, and beaches generally make more attractive places to live than flat nondescript barren areas. In addition to aesthetics, consider the functional implications of geography. Living on a mountain provides more than just a view. It also keeps a home well above the flood waters which may accumulate in the valley below.

Government Forces

Local government has an impact on the value of real estate as a result of its intervention in the marketplace. The primary government actions which affect the value of a home include capital improvements, zoning, and comprehensive land use planning.

Capital improvements are those construction projects undertaken by local government to support and/or stimulate development activity. Examples include building and renovating schools; building and widening roads; building parks; developing new water and sewer treatment facilities, and other such projects. Capital improvements generally have a positive impact on home values. Local governments finance capital improvements through bond issues, loans, and cash out of their capital budgets. The revenues to pay for these improvements generally come from property taxes, sales taxes, use taxes, and income taxes, as well as revenue received from state and federal government subsidies and grants.

Local governments have a capital improvements plan and before buying a home you should examine this plan. It will show the schools, roads, parks and other public projects planned in an area for the next five to ten years. If numerous improvements are planned, then it is often a good strategy to be one of the first home buyers in the area and thus put yourself in a position to realize a value increase when the planned improvements are completed.

For example, if new schools and parks are planned, but not yet developed, you would be wise to locate near these planned improvements and position yourself to enjoy the future benefits they will provide. This only makes sense, however, if the capital improvements are funded and will be completed in a short time frame, such as one to three years.

Government also influences the market through comprehensive land use planning and zoning regulations. The intent of such regulation is to protect property values and the health and safety of citizens. Zoning regulations typically prohibit a power plant or heavy manufacturing facility from being developed too near a residential area, for such an industrial use would not be consistent with residential development and could pose a danger to residents and their property.

Land use plans typically divide a neighborhood into district classifications, such as single family residential districts (houses), multifamily residential districts (apartments and condominiums), commercial districts (office and retail centers), industrial districts (warehouses, manufacturing and utility plants), and recreational/conservation districts (parks, lakes, streams and other such areas).

A well designed land use plan will place transition zones between high and low intensity uses as follows:

Single Family Residential

Multifamily Residential

Recreation/Conservation

Office

Retail

Light Industrial

Heavy Industrial

As can be seen, residential uses are shielded from potentially dangerous industrial uses by transitional zones comprised of recreation/conservation, office and retail districts.

Before buying a home, examine land use plans and zoning maps. These will govern the future uses which can be legally developed near your property. It is wise to seek a home in an area surrounded by residential and recreation/conservation uses, for such a strategy will ensure compatible development and use conformity, as well as provide close recreation and scenic buffers.

Avoid buying a home in a transitional area where land uses change from one type to another, especially if the changing uses are intense. For example, avoid buying a home adjacent to or very near commercial and industrial districts. Being too close to these uses will subject your home to increased traffic, congestion, pollution, noise and other nuisances.

Summary

In summary, a neighborhood is a subsection of a larger overall area which has a unique character. There are wealthy neighborhoods, modest neighborhoods, growing neighborhoods, declining neighborhoods, etc. When evaluating these subsections, thoroughly research the economic, social, geographic, and governmental forces within them, for these forces will impact future property values and quality of life.

4. HOMESITES

A homesite consists of the parcel of land underlying a home. Whether you are evaluating the homesite of an existing home or a homesite for new development, there are specific types and features you should consider. This chapter will discuss these important criteria.

Types of Homesites

Basically, there are three types of homesites; urban, suburban, and rural. Urban homesites are located within the heart of metropolitan areas and are generally referred to as being "in the city" (but not necessarily "inner city"). Suburban homesites are those located on the outer fringes of urban areas, typically along roadway systems between the city and the country. And lastly, rural homesites are those located outside of the influence of a major metropolitan area and are generally referred to as being "in the country."

Most urban and suburban homesites are developed within planned (platted) communities called subdivisions, which are created when a developer "subdivides" a parcel of land into smaller units called lots. Typically, lots share common size and shape features and tend to have a high degree of conformity. This feature serves to keep values somewhat uniform. For example, lots in a particular subdivision may average 0.30 acres in size with a width of 110 feet and a depth of 120 feet, and the average lot price may range from $30,000 to $32,500 depending on corner or interior orientation.

The subdivision process begins when a developer takes a plan called a "plat" to local government officials for approval. The plat describes the subdivision and shows all the lots which will be developed on the tract of land. It reveals the dimensions, flood zone and elevation of the lots; the placement of planned roadways, utilities, easements, drainage routes and ponds; applicable deed restrictions, and other such features. After getting the plat approved, it is recorded in the public records and development begins.

In rural areas, most homesites are not part of platted subdivisions. Instead, they typically consist of tracts which have been "cut out" of farms and other large land holdings. Such homesites do not share the common size and character features of subdivided lots. They are generally larger than one acre in size. The large size is a direct relationship of the cost of land, for land in the country is typically less expensive than land in urban and suburban areas. Thus, a home buyer can buy more land for the money in the country.

Physical Features

Important physical features to consider when evaluating a homesite include size, shape, topography, view, and vegetation.

The appropriate size of a homesite is a function of individual preference. Large lots generally spread houses apart and provide more privacy and seclusion, while small lots bring houses closer together and promote social interaction among residents. When evaluating size, recognize these trends. If you are terribly shy and reclusive, then a large lot is a better choice, for the interaction with neighbors created by small lots may be too hard on your psyche. If you enjoy social interaction, then avoid large lots which may leave you isolated from neighbors.

If you decide to buy a small lot and you have kids, then make sure a park or square is nearby. This is very important if the boundaries of the lot restrict the ability of kids to play baseball, kickball, or other such games in the yard. A nearby park which can be accessed via a sidewalk system can provide the needed playground, for you don't want the kids playing in the street. Therefore, if a park is present, you can buy in a neighborhood where houses are close together so as to maximize your ability to meet neighbors, develop strong social ties, and keep land costs low, while also having a safe open place where kids can gather and play.

The shape of a homesite is important. The best shapes are rectangles and squares, and the worst are highly irregular shapes. Rectangles and squares provide good frontage to depth ratios and create a highly developable area. In contrast, irregular shapes may pose development problems associated with setback and minimum yard requirements. Generally, interior lots are rectangular with a width less than depth; corner lots are more square shaped; and parcels along cul-de-sacs are pie shaped. These shapes influence the features of the home which will be built upon the site.

For example, a corner lot provides a home with a high degree of visibility and exposure, but less privacy, while a pie shaped lot provides a home with less visibility and exposure, but more privacy. Choose the shape which meets your desires, but avoid shapes which create development problems.

A highly functional homesite should contain three zones; public, service, and private zones. The public zone is the front yard and it provides a buffer against the noise and dangers of the street. The service zone is the area along the sides of a site where cars and boats are parked, and where trashcans and yard equipment can be stored. The private zone is the area behind the house where cookouts, swimming, and recreational activities can take place out of view of the public. Therefore, make sure the lot size and shape provide adequate area for each zone.

Elevation (height of the property above sea level) affects the desirability of a homesite. In Florida, most homesites have an elevation of less than 100 feet, while in mountainous areas such as Colorado elevations may be several thousand feet above sea level. This does not mean, however, that lots in Colorado are superior to lots in Florida, all other features being equal.

The main point to consider with respect to elevation is "relative elevation." By this I mean the elevation of a property relative to the elevation of adjoining properties. It is wise to purchase a homesite at an elevation which is higher than the elevation of adjoining properties. In this way, you can ensure drainage occurs away from (not to) your property, thus leaving you "high and dry" in times of heavy rains and melting snows. This does not mean you have to live on a mountain top, for you can achieve this result by purchasing a homesite with an elevation of 50 feet when surrounding properties have elevations ranging from 25 to 30 feet.

Grade is the slope of a property and it affects value by influencing the drainage and development potential of a homesite. There are two extremes of grade; no slope (totally flat and level) and radical slope (a steep incline or decline such as along a mountain side). Building a home on these two extremes may require special site preparation and foundational costs, above and beyond the norm. In particular, a totally level grade will not drain, and if the soil doesn't percolate well rainwater may pool, settle and stagnate. Building on such a homesite should include elevating the foundation, building up the driveway, and creating a slope to lead water towards a retention pond or drainage canal/ditch.

At the opposite extreme, a radically sloping grade such as an extreme incline or decline on a mountain face can cause difficulty in constructing a safe and secure home. Homes on such slopes typically are built upon pilings driven into the ground.

Mud slides, rock slides, earthquakes, erosion and avalanches pose danger to homes on extreme grades.

The best grade to look for in a homesite is a slight decline away from the house. This grade provides drainage and a enhanced view. The change in grade should be subtle enough so as to not create construction problems or restrict the use of the back yard for recreational purposes, yet steep enough to move water away from the house.

To determine the grade and elevation of a property first go examine it in relation to adjacent properties. A thorough visual inspection can identify many potential problems. Next, go to the local library and look at topographical (topo) maps prepared by the United States Department of the Interior, Geological Survey. These maps cover fairly large areas and show property elevations, as well as the presence of waterways. The following is an excerpt of a topo map of an area.

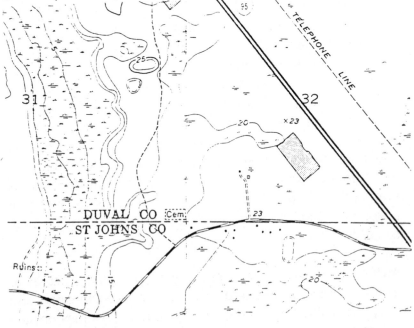

Topographical Map

Examine flood insurance rate maps prepared by the United States Flood Emergency Management Agency (FEMA). A copy of these maps is usually available free of charge at local city and county building departments. The maps will show which properties are within the 100 year flood plain, and which are located outside of the 500 year flood plain. Avoid buying a homesite inside the flood plain, for this will greatly reduce the risk of flood damage and the cost of flood insurance.

Lastly, go to your local library or map service and examine the National Wetland Inventory Maps for the area. These maps identify wetland systems, including system type and boundaries. It is important to note wetland areas near or on a homesite, for wetlands are highly regulated by the government and protected for the public welfare. As such, they cannot be developed or impacted in any way without special permits. As a result, wetlands are generally considered "untouchable lands."

Though topographical surveys, topographical maps, flood maps and wetland maps are all good sources of information, probably the best method of evaluation is to visit a homesite after periods of heavy sustained rains. If large amounts of standing water and flooding are found, avoid buying. However, if no water can be found, even though other areas of town are flooded, then this is a good indication the property is well drained.

The view a lot provides is an important aesthetic and enjoyment feature to consider. Some lots provide a fantastic view, such as the scenery of an open expansive valley from the side or top of a mountain; the scenery of a long sandy beach and rolling ocean waves; or the scenery of a large quiet lake from a wooded hillside. Other lots don't afford much of a view, and may be limited to a few trees or the neighbor's backyard. In general, the better the view, the more expensive the homesite, and, likewise, the poorer the view the cheaper the homesite.

For those lots which afford a view, there are some important feature to research before spending the premium dollars involved. If the lot adjoins a lake, river or other freshwater body, then research the quality of the water to make sure it is fit for swimming, fishing, and other recreational activities. This can be accomplished by contacting state and local government agencies or environmental groups and obtaining information regarding the specific waterway.

For example, I obtained a map from a state agency in Florida known as the St. Johns River Water Management District. This District governs all waters within the St. Johns River basin, a huge area extending from Jacksonville to Melbourne along Florida's east coast. The map pertains to waters within the Jacksonville area, and classifies these waters by quality; i.e., good, threatened, fair, and poor. Typically, the areas classified as fair or poor are subjected to a source of pollution, such as industry or treated sewage. As such, it would be wise to avoid buying a homesite and paying a lot of money for a parcel adjoining poor water.

If buying a home with a view of the coastline, beware of coastal setback requirements. These federal and state regulations limit the distance a home can be placed in proximity to the mean high water mark, the dune line, and other designated boundaries. This is a critical consideration, for some home buyers have paid in excess of $100,000 for a beach front lot only to discover later the lot is not readily buildable due to these regulatory boundaries. Also, some insurance companies will no longer insure homes along the coast as a result of recent heavy losses from hurricanes, which seem to strike every few years with catastrophic economic consequences. Therefore, if shopping for a beach front homesite, keep these factors in mind.

The quality and design of public access to a property affects its value and appeal. Most home buyers seek paved, publicly main tained roads leading to and from their homesite, and the paving surface of choice is usually asphalt or concrete. These surfaces are hardy, easy to maintain, and have a fairly long physical life. Access should be publicly maintained so that tax dollars pay for maintenance and resurfacing. Otherwise, you and other residents will be responsible for coughing up the money for repair and re-paving expenses, which can be significant.

I generally recommend living along a narrow, curved, tree lined, non-thru street which does not provide access to other areas. Traffic along such streets is typically light and restricted to residents and visitors, thus maximizing peace and security. Such a design also precludes people from racing through a subdivision as a short cut to another place, and this is especially important to families with young children and pets. The following plat of a subdivision illustrates this concept. Note: there is only one entrance and the streets do not lead to other areas.

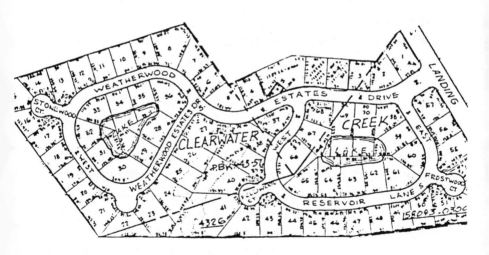

Street Network in a Subdivision

If you have young children, then sidewalks are important. Sidewalks keep kids from walking, riding and skating in the streets, thus adding a good measure of safety. They should be paved and traverse parallel a safe distance from the street, and they should be placed in the front public yard of homes. Sidewalks should not be in rear yard areas where kids can be assaulted out of sight of the street. Lastly, sidewalks should lead to all destinations of importance to children, such as schools and play-grounds.

A good quality subdivision should also be enclosed with perimeter fencing or natural barriers. Such distinct boundaries reduce crime and increase privacy. Good natural barriers include rivers, lakes, and swamps, which also add to the view and attractiveness of an area. Good perimeter fencing includes concrete or brick walls. Walls should be at least six feet in height. Wood fencing is not a good barrier in my opinion, for over time it rots and becomes unattractive, and can be broken through easily with heavy hammers.

Utilities

All homesites should be located within close proximity to public electric and telephone service. If these services are not adjacent to the homesite, don't assume the utility company will extend them free of charge. I recently heard of a couple who sold their house in the city and retired to the country. They bought an old farmhouse on a big acreage tract and set about renovating it. The farmhouse didn't have electricity or phone service, so they went to the local electric and phone companies and asked them to extend service to the house. The utility companies agreed, but extension costs exceeded $100,000; more than they paid for the entire property. Faced with such a cost, they were forced to sell the farmhouse and seek a residence closer into town. Avoid such situations and only consider a homesite served by electric and phone lines.

Proximity to public water and sewer service is also important, but less critical in areas which allow the development of a well and septic tank system. In most rural areas, there are no nearby water and sewer systems, so wells and septic tanks are required. Installing a well and septic system is initially more expensive than connecting with public systems and can cost several thousands of dollars. However, once installed, such systems have no monthly service fee (other than minor electricity charges). In contrast, public water and sewer systems can have a fairly expensive monthly fee. One drawback: septic tanks require periodic pumping and both the well and septic tank require periodic maintenance.

As stated, public water and sewer systems are cheaper to access, but have a monthly service fee, which includes a base charge as well as a user charge (based on gallons of water consumed). I prefer public water and sewer systems over well and septic systems even though they cost more, for the homeowner is not responsible for any maintenance costs or quality concerns. In addition, if public water systems are available, then there are most likely fire hydrants nearby. This, in turn, will reduce homeowners insurance costs.

Zoning and Restrictions

Basic zoning information was presented in the chapter on neighborhoods. However, in this chapter, I want to expand the discussion of this topic to include the impact of zoning on homesites.

When checking the zoning of a property there are two primary things you should research:

1) Permissible uses
2) Physical constraints

Permissible uses within a zoning category include those uses which can be legally developed. In a single family residential zoning district, permissible uses may be limited to single family homes and some minor ancillary uses such as daycare centers and essential services. This zoning typically precludes multifamily, commercial and industrial development. Don't buy a homesite in a zoning district which allows commercial or industrial uses, or you may wake up one morning to find a shopping center or office building being constructed next door.

Physical constraints of zoning pertain to minimum lot sizes, minimum lot widths, maximum lot coverage ratios, and setbacks. The minimum lot size and lot width requirements are self explanatory and require a homesite be a specific size and width, or greater, to be developed. Most residential zonings require a minimum lot width of from 80 to 125 feet. Such minimum widths help ensure lots will have a good shape and productive frontage-to-depth ratio, as well as sufficient space on the side yard between homes.

The size requirement ties in with density of allowable housing development, which is often expressed in terms of units per acre. For instance, a zoning with a maximum density of 4 units per acre often has a minimum lot size of roughly 10,000 square feet (allowing some area for the development of roadways and infrastructure). The lower the density the bigger the lots, and the higher the density the smaller the lots.

Maximum lot coverage ratios pertain to how much of the homesite can be developed. For example, if the zoning specifies a maximum lot coverage ratio of 20% and the homesite contains 10,000 square feet, then the maximum footprint area (foundation area) of the home cannot exceed 2,000 square feet (10,000 square feet x 20% = 2,000 square feet). Such restrictions attempt to avoid overcrowding a homesite.

Setback requirements pertain to how far the house must be setback from the boundaries of the homesite. This includes front, side and rear yard setbacks. For example, the front yard setback may be 25 feet, the side yard setbacks 15 feet, and the rear yard setback 10 feet. Such restrictions ensure a home isn't built too close to a road or too close to a neighboring property to ensure privacy and safety.

Deed restrictions are also important legal considerations affecting the value of a homesite. A deed restriction is a special clause which a seller includes as part of the deed to a property. Such restrictions are called private restrictions because they are established by private parties (developers, homeowners, etc.), as opposed to public parties (the government). Deed restrictions are very common in subdivisions and are present to control the type of homes which are built. Examples of deed restrictions may include the following:

- Restrictions as to the minimum home size allowed; i.e., the home shall be greater than or equal to 1,800 square feet.

- Restrictions as to architectural standards. This typically pertains to styles, colors, materials, and interior finishes; i.e., the home shall be built with an exterior siding of brick or stucco, colors shall be limited to colonial tones per the ACME architectural guide, etc.

- Restrictions precluding certain types of homes and uses; i.e., no mobile homes allowed, no farm animals shall be kept on the property, no clotheslines shall be allowed in the front yard, no fences shall be installed in the front yard, no above ground pools shall be installed, no park ing of boats or recreational vehicles in the yard, no work ing on automobiles in the front yard, and similar type restrictions.

Carefully researching zoning laws and deed restrictions is critical, for it is my experience that development will occur to the lowest common denominator. For example, I know of several cases where large stately homes were developed along a beautifully scenic river or lake. However, no deed restrictions were present, and, as a result, much smaller homes were developed across the street. This radically inconsistent development pattern eroded the value of the waterfront homes. Therefore, protect your investment by looking for a homesite in an area with zoning and deed restrictions which regulate development, provide conformity, and ensure the quality of lifestyle you are seeking.

Architectural Review

If a community is governed by deed restrictions involving architectural standards, then a designated architectural review person or committee must approve all plans prior to construction or local government agencies will not grant a building permit. This process helps preserve the quality and integrity of a community. For example, I serve on the Architectural Modification and Advisory Committee (AMAC) of a 4,100 acre master planned community. Our committee reviews all structural additions and modifications to existing homes.

The AMAC seeks to maintain development within the constraints of established guidelines designed to preserve the high quality development. Such review committees are good for the long term health of a community.

Homeowner's Associations

If you are evaluating a homesite within a subdivision or condominium project, be sure to find out if a homeowner's association is present. Homeowner's associations are established so that common areas will continue to be maintained after development is complete. In reference to subdivisions, the process works as follows:

When a developer begins a new subdivision, he pays all the costs of building and maintaining the common areas, which may include a landscaped entranceway, security fencing, clubhouse, pool, and other such amenities. Then, as the developer sells lots, he transfers a percentage of ownership in these common areas to the new owners. Along with ownership comes liability for a share of the cost of maintenance. In this way, a developer transfers all his interest and liability in the common areas to the lot owners via deed clauses. When all lots are sold, the developer leaves, and the lot owners become responsible for all maintenance, upkeep, and liability.

For example, assume a subdivision contains 100 lots and is improved with a guard house for security, and common amenities consisting of a pool, clubhouse, and tennis courts. These areas are called "common" because all residents in the subdivision have the right to use and benefit from them. The cost of maintaining these common areas is $100,000 a year.

The developer establishes a homeowner's association to handle these costs and concerns in the future. When he sells a lot, a 1% interest (1 lot/100 lots = 1%) in the homeowner's association is transferred to the new lot owner. Thus, the new lot owner becomes responsible for paying 1% of the annual maintenance cost of $100,000, or $1,000 a year. After selling all 100 lots, the homeowner's association is made up entirely of new lot owners and the developer no longer has an ownership interest in the property.

If you buy into an association and amenities include items such as a playground, pool or lake, then make sure an excellent liability insurance policy is in-place to protect against claims associated with injury or death on common grounds. Also, make sure insurance is present to cover the replacement cost of improvements in case of fire, storm, vandalism or other damage.

If common areas include major structures such as a clubhouse, then the association should also set aside funds every year for the periodic replacement of short lived building components; i.e., money to replace the roof, carpet and air conditioner, for these items will wear out over time. Establishing such a reserve and planning ahead will eliminate the need for costly special assessments when repairs are required.

For example, assume carpet costs are ± $2.00/square foot. If a clubhouse contains 2,000 square feet, then the cost to replace the carpet will be approximately $4,000 (2,000 Sq. Ft. x $2.00/Sq. Ft.). Carpet typically has a useful life of 7 years. If the association puts aside $500 per year in a bank account earning 4% interest per year, then the account will grow to roughly $4,000 in seven years. In this manner, funds will be available to replace the carpet when needed. However, if no such reserve is set aside, then residents will be forced with raising $4,000 through a special assessment. The same holds true for replacing the roof, HVAC unit, pool liner, tennis court surface, etc.

Lastly, though homeowners associations can be rife with politics, don't let this frighten you away. Homeowners associations are established for the good of homeowners, such as yourself. They serve as a means of getting to know neighbors, establishing lifelong friendships, and maintaining the quality of your community. The homeowner's association of which my family is part sponsors parties at special times of the year for children; maintains a first rate recreational complex with pools, parks and soccer fields; and keeps the extensive landscaping trim and neat. The association's members work hard on donated time to make the community an enjoyable and beautiful place to live.

Legal Descriptions

When evaluating a homesite it is important to know its legal description. Such a description is the legal means of establishing the boundaries and location of a property. Only experienced lawyers and surveyors should be involved in preparing legal descriptions, but every buyer should know how to read them.

Describing a property in legally acceptable terms is sometimes difficult. Just saying a property's boundaries go from a big oak tree to a tall skinny pine tree, and then over to a boulder with an X on it doesn't suffice like it did 100 years ago. What would happen if one of the landmark trees was blown down in a storm or burned up in a fire, or if one of your crafty neighbors moved the boulder marked by an X to make your property smaller and his bigger? Such problems occurred in older days prior to the advent of our current systems of describing properties.

A legal description is important because it lets everyone know the boundaries of a property. As such, a basic understanding of legal descriptions is beneficial.

The following are the three methods of legally describing parcels of real estate today:

1) Lot and Block System (for subdivisions)

2) Government Survey System (for non-subdivided properties)

3) Metes and Bounds System (for non-subdivided properties)

A subdivided homesite is usually legally described using the lot and block system. The exact physical dimensions of the lot cannot be ascertained from the legal description itself, but are incorporated by reference to a recorded plat. Therefore, if you buy a lot in a subdivision, I recommend getting a copy of the plat for your files. An example of a lot and block legal description is as follows:

Lot 1, Block A, Lake Asbury Subdivision, as recorded within Plat Book 5, Page 45, of the public records of Clay County, Florida.

Someone seeking to know the dimensions and exact location of this lot would go to the local public records office; look up Page 5 of Plat Book 45 to find the Lake Asbury Subdivision; and look for Lot 1. This plat would then show the dimensions, flood zone, road placement, and other features of the homesite. The following is a copy of part of a plat showing the dimensions of a lot in a subdivision.

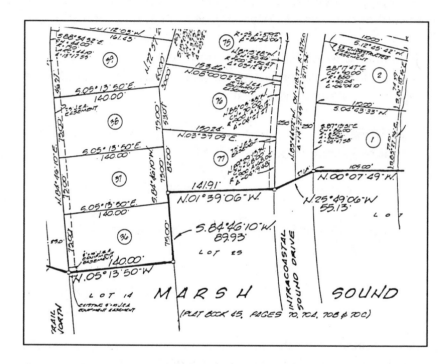

Plat of Lots in a Subdivision

The government survey system is another form of legal description and is based on a grid of longitudinal (north-south) lines called range lines and latitudinal (east-west) lines called township lines. These longitudinal and latitudinal lines crisscross to form 6 mile square areas called townships. Each township contains 36 one square mile subareas called sections, and each section contains 640 acres.

An example of a government survey legal description may read as follows:

> The Northwest quarter of the Northeast quarter of the Northeast quarter of the Northwest quarter of Section 15, Township 1 North, Range 26 East, Duval County, Florida.

In the above example, the lot size is 2.5 acres, for it is the fourth root of 640 acres comprising a Section, i.e. 640 acres ÷ 4 ÷ 4 ÷ 4 ÷ 4 = 2.5 acres. Rural homesites are often described using the government survey system.

A metes and bounds description is the last type of legal description, and it is based on directions and distances, as well as reference to landmarks. In older times, it included reference to stakes, monuments, and physical landmarks. Today, surveying equipment and satellite assistance are used to pinpoint locations to degrees, minutes and seconds on a map. An example of how a metes and bounds description may be written is as follows:

> Commencing at the Northeast intersection of Maple Street and Oak Street; thence North 90 degrees East a distance of 100 feet along the northerly right of way of Maple Street to the Point of Beginning; thence continue North 90 degrees East a distance of 100 feet; thence North 0 degrees East a distance of 100 feet; thence North 90 degrees West a distance of 100 feet; and then South 0 degrees East a distance of 100 feet to the Point of Beginning.

The above describes a square parcel with the dimensions of 100 feet by 100 feet, thus containing a gross area of 10,000 square feet (100 x 100 = 10,000).

Government survey and metes and bounds legal descriptions are often applied together and an example of such a description is as follows:

> Part of Section 1, Township 3 South, Range 27 East, Duval County, Florida, beginning at the southeast corner of Section 1 marked by a concrete monument; thence North 90 degrees East 100 feet, thence due South 100 feet, thence North 90 degrees West 100 feet, thence due North 100 feet to the point of beginning.

Summary

In summary, a homesite consists of a parcel of land underlying a home, and, basically, there are three types of homesites; urban, suburban and rural. Most urban and suburban homesites are located within platted subdivisions and share common characteristics, while most rural homesites are more unique and have been "cut out" of farms, forests, and other large parcels.

Important features to consider in a homesite are size, shape, elevation, grade, topography, view, access, utilities, zoning and deed restrictions. Lastly, it is helpful to understand the legal methods of describing homesites, and these methods include lot and block, metes and bounds, and government survey.

5. HOME DESIGN

Every potential home buyer should be aware of the basic housing alternatives available in the marketplace and have an understanding of the precepts of good design.

HOUSING TYPES

Basically, there are two types of housing; detached and attached. A detached home is an individual unit, separate from any other housing unit. The following is a picture of a detached home:

Single Family Detached Home

In contrast, attached homes share a common wall. The following is a photograph of attached housing units, in this case condominium units:

Attached Home

Your choice of housing type should be a function of lifestyle needs and budget constraints. Detached units include houses and patio homes. Patio homes are also known as zero lot line homes, for they have very little yard (lot area). Attached housing units include condominiums, apartments, row houses, townhouses, etc.

Generally, attached homes are less expensive than comparable size detached homes, for they include less land and share at least one common wall. Attached housing typically has little-to-no yard or exterior maintenance concerns, thus allowing more time and money to pursue other interests. However, if you have kids, then a detached home with a yard may be a better choice.

Home Zones

A well designed home, like a properly designed site, should be divided into three distinct zones; the service, social and private zones. The service zone is the noisy work area where cooking, laundering, and other work activities take place. This zone typically consists of the garage, utility/laundry room, kitchen and hobby room. These areas contain the heavy appliances, machinery and fixtures which generate noise, heat and odors; i.e., ovens, clothes washers, clothes dryers, water heaters, and power tools. The service zone should be clearly separated from the social and private zones. This is logical not only from a noise and energy reduction point of view, but also for safety considerations.

The social zone is the part of the home where family members and guests congregate to dine, visit, watch television, and enjoy other social/entertainment activities. This zone typically consists of the dining room, living room, breakfast nook, and family room/den. These rooms are generally the largest within the home.

The last zone is the private zone. It is the area containing the bedrooms and bathrooms, and is the place where family and guests sleep, bathe, and perform other private functions. It should be the quietest and most secluded area. For fire safety and other health considerations, this zone should be buffered from the service zone by the social zone.

A well designed floor plan should provide each of these zones, as well as a distinct separation between them. This concept is illustrated by the following floor plan:

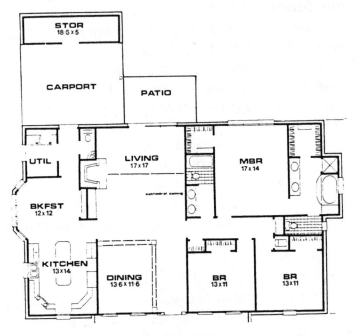

Well Zoned Floor Plan

As can be seen, in this ranch style floor plan, zones transition from service to social to private. Each is distinct and self-contained. Such a layout allows the private zone to be well insulated from the noise and potential hazards of the service zone, yet also places the dining room and breakfast nook (social zones) near the kitchen (service zone) so food and drink can be easily served.

It should be noted that many modern homes are being designed with a split floor plan in which the master bedroom is placed on one side or floor of the home while the other bedrooms are placed on the opposite side or floor. As with any design, there are pros and cons to such an arrangement. The pros include maximizing the privacy of the owners/parents. Cons include placement of bedrooms near the service zone and the inability to closely monitor activities in other bedrooms. An example of a split floor plan follows:

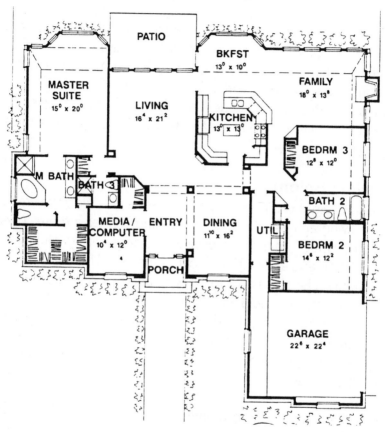

Split Floor Plan

A well designed home should have at least one point of access per zone. Most homes have a garage and side door leading from the service zone of the homesite into the service zone of the kitchen and laundry room. Also, most have a decorative front door leading from the social zone of the homesite into the social zone of the house, such as the living and dining area. This front door is typically reserved for guests and company, and is not used by residents on a daily basis. However, not all homes have access points in the private zone. A door providing access from the private zone to the outside should be installed as a fire and emergency escape.

When analyzing a floor plan, look for visual and noise barriers between zones, such as hallways, closets and walls. Optimally, a resident should be able to go from the bedroom to the bathroom and back again without being seen by anyone in the social zone. In addition, a guest should be able to use a restroom in privacy without being seen entering the facility from the social or service areas.

Ceiling Height

Ceiling height can have a significant effect on the visual impact of a living area. A 10 to 12 foot ceiling creates a more "open, luxurious feel" than the typical 8 to 9 foot ceiling. During the late 1800s and early 1900s, most of the grand homes of the era had ceiling heights of 12 to 14 feet, and included accents such as ornate crown molding. After the depression of the 1930s, ceilings in most homes became more modest, and heights shrank to 8 and 9 feet. However, modern homes are once again capturing the charm and luxury of old world homes by implementing this feature.

To enjoy this effect, yet minimize cost, many homes have 10 foot ceilings in the social zones of the living room, dining room, family room and nook, but the remaining portions of the house, including the bedrooms and bathrooms, have 8 foot ceilings.

Orientation

The sun rises in the east and sets in the west, and it's trajectory is higher in the sky during the summer months than during the winter months. Recognizing this daily and seasonal pattern, it is possible to enhance the energy efficiency and climate control functions of a home via good site placement. Specifically, by placing the broad sides of a home in a north/south position, more area can be exposed to the heat of the sun during the low trajectory winter months, resulting in lower heating costs. Also, installing overhangs from the eaves, the broad side of the home can be shaded from the direct rays of the sun during the high trajectory summer months, thus lowering cooling costs. This concept is illustrated below:

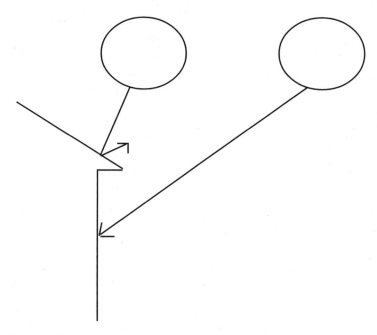

House Placement and Sun Trajectory

Such energy enhancement is not achieved if the broad side of a home is placed in an east/west position. In this orientation, the broad side of the house bears the brunt of the hot summer sun in the afternoon, increasing cooling costs. Also, in this orientation, only the narrow sides of the home are exposed to the warming effects of the winter sun, thus increases heating costs. Therefore, orient a home in a north/south position to maximize energy efficiency.

Recognizing the impact of the sun's trajectory on the comfort and energy costs associated with a home, it is possible to design a home to counter the sun's effect. For example, in southern climates where heat is a primary concern, a well designed home will include a garage along the west wall to buffer the living area from the effects of the afternoon sun. In this way, the garage serves as insulation.

Another important design consideration is proper room placement. To maximize comfort and reduce energy costs, it is often helpful to place rooms used in the morning, such as the breakfast room, away from the east side of the home which bears the brunt of the early day sun. Likewise, it is often helpful to place rooms used in the afternoon and evening, such as the bedrooms and dining area, away from the west face of the home, which bears the brunt of the afternoon sun. Social zones such as the family and living rooms are best placed in the center of the home well insulated from the effects of the sun.

The number of stories of a home is another important consideration. Heat rises. Therefore, many homes in Northern climates are built of at least two stories with the private zones (bedrooms and bathrooms) upstairs to maximize warmth. Formerly homes in the South were also two story structures, but for a different reason; to elevate the living area in an attempt to capture as much breeze as possible. With the advent of air conditioning, this is no longer as critical, and most Southern homes are built as single story structures with high roof lines to separate the rising heat from the living area. Taking into consideration these design features can significantly affect your comfort level and energy costs.

Health implications should also be considered when evaluating a multistory design. Stairs can be difficult, if not impossible, to climb for some elderly individuals and those with weak knees, ankles, etc. Also, stairs can be dangerous for young children.

Cases of toddlers falling down stairs and suffering severe or fatal injuries are all too common. Therefore, if your household includes elderly, very young children, or those with weak legs, then a multistory home is probably not the best choice, even though the "look" appeals to you.

This brings up an important point; many families buy a home based on its look and appeal, rather than looking beyond the surface and considering all the design, construction, and other features. Just like buying a car, appearances can be deceiving. You must look "under the hood." Be an informed consumer/ investor and know what you want before buying.

The overall size of a home is an important consideration, and is usually a factor of finances; not choice. But size directly influences the way a home feels. The goal should be to avoid a cramped situation in which the walls appear to be closing in on you, yet maximize your investment dollars by purchasing only what you need. There are some who buy extremely large and opulent homes to make a statement of their success and status, but, as will be discussed in later chapters, this is rarely wise from a monetary investment point of view.

Most homes have a separate formal dining room. Such rooms should be placed near, but not part of, the food preparation area. Thus, they are different from nooks, which are typically part of the kitchen. Ideally, the dining room should be large enough to comfortably sit guests and family around a table while including room for other furnishings such as a China Closet, buffet, etc. Generally, dimensions of at least 10 feet by 12 feet (±120 square feet) are adequate.

In homes with separate formal living and family rooms, the living room is generally smaller than the family room. Dimensions of at least 10 feet by 12 feet (120 square feet) are adequate. The living room is often used just for intimate entertaining.

The family room is more casual in nature and is the place family and close friends relax, visit, watch television, etc. This room will typically be the largest in the home with dimensions of at least 16 feet by 14 feet (±225 square feet).

Today, many modern homes do not include formal living rooms, for society has become more casual. Instead, the formal living area is often absorbed by the family room to create a large "great room." Such a combined room is generally oval or rectangular in shape with dimensions of at least 18 feet by 18 feet (±360 square feet). Great rooms should allow enough area for the comfortable placement of couches, chairs and entertainment equipment such as a television, VCR, and stereo.

Kitchen shapes vary, but a well designed one will allow enough room for free movement and access to appliances and current trends are toward bigger and more open kitchens. Dimensions of at least 8 feet by 10 feet (±80 square feet) are generally adequate in small to medium sized homes.

As mentioned, kitchens are becoming more open and part of the social area of a home. As such, they tend to flow into adjoining nooks and great rooms allowing the cook to watch kids or visit with guests while preparing meals. Such a design often includes a bar and half wall which allows a clear view between rooms.

Most kitchens are designed around the triangle concept in which the sink, refrigerator/freezer, and stove/range each form a point of the triangle and are located on separate walls. The points of the triangle should be close together so the cook can bounce freely and frequently between them with ease. The following diagram illustrates this concept.

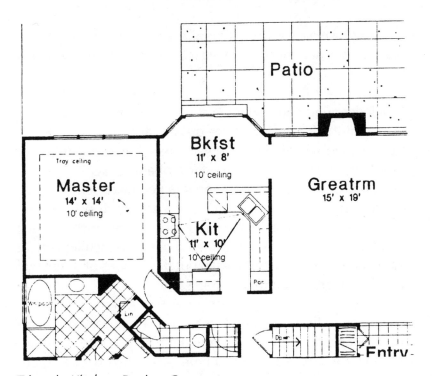

Triangle Kitchen Design Concept

Master bedrooms are typically bigger than other bedrooms and the market often dictates they include a private attached bathroom. Dimensions of at least 12 feet by 14 feet (±170 square feet) are typical, with rooms of at least 14 feet by 14 feet (±200 square feet) preferred. Regular bedrooms, on the other hand, are smaller. The minimum size should be at least 10 feet by 12 feet (±120 square feet), with sizes of at least 12 feet by 12 feet (±150 square feet) preferred.

Bathrooms are growing more spacious and elegant, with many master baths including large garden tubs and separately enclosed showers. Many include a vanity (sink and dressing area) separated from the toilet and shower areas. This allows multi-use capability, for one spouse can get dressed in the vanity area relatively unaffected by the hot steamy shower being taken by the other spouse. Guest bathrooms are generally rectangular in shape and smaller in size. Typical dimensions are based on a five foot tub, and most are at least 5 feet by 10 feet (50 square feet).

A well designed home should have a foyer. This is a small area located at the front door where guests can enter a home without stepping directly into a public area. Foyers are transition areas between the outside and inside where guests are greeted, and coats can be taken and hung in a nearby closet. Most foyers are designed to welcome guests to a home and include prime floor coverings, a nice entry lamp (often a small chandelier), and an attractive front door. Dimensions vary depending on the statement being made to guests, but dimensions of 7 feet by 5 feet (35 square feet) are adequate.

In addition to the basic rooms discussed, a well designed home will include a laundry room, cupboard/pantry, and adequate closet space. It is important to note that recent discoveries reveal a clothes dryer is the primary threat to indoor comfort levels. Specifically, a dryer works like a reverse heating unit. It sucks air in from the home, heats it, blows the hot air over the clothes, and then expels the used air through a vent to the outside. Most dryers run for at least 30 minutes to an hour per cycle, and during this time they have the capacity to suck all the cold or warm air out of an 1,800 square foot home and vent it outside. This creates several problems.

First, your air conditioner or heater must run to replace the cold or hot air which has been "sucked out" and, secondly, since the dryer is sucking air out of the home, this lost air must be replaced with other air since homes are never air tight. If they were air tight, a vacuum would result in which all air is sucked out of a home, eventually causing an implosion. However, since homes are not air tight, new air is generally sucked in out of the attic, interior wall partitions, and cracks in the wall/ceiling gaps. This "sucked in" air from structural cavities is generally contaminated with insulation, dust, mold and mildew, causing a definite health concern. Since the air is not being sucked into the home via the air conditioner/heater, it is not filtered or heated/cooled when it enters the home.

One way to avoid the unpleasant side effects of operating a clothes dryer is to place the appliance outside the living area; i.e., in the garage. At a minimum, place it in a self contained laundry room equipped with a window. This window should be opened when the dryer is in operation so that air is sucked in through the window to the unit, and the air in the home can remain, for the most part, unaffected. This concept of air movement and its health and energy implications will be more fully discussed in the section on air conditioning systems.

The same concept applies to the location of the air handler unit. Despite what many codes state, air handlers should be placed inside the living area. This serves two functions. First, it minimizes the threat of introducing dangerous chemicals, dust or germs from the garage and attic in the event a duct leak occurs. Second, it reduces the amount of duct work exposed to outside air temperatures; optimizing energy efficiency. This concept will be more fully discussed in later chapters.

The pantry should be located adjacent to the kitchen, and is basically a closet designed to store food and staples. It generally includes either shelves or cabinets, and may be open to the kitchen, or separately enclosed via a door.

With regard to general closet space, all bedrooms should include a closet with rack and shelves. The closet in the master bedroom is often a large walk-in type; sometimes two (one for each spouse). There should also be a closet in or near the guest bathroom to store towels and linens. It is important to design a home so that closets perform two functions; storage and sound buffer. To realize the second function, closets should be placed between bedrooms and adjoining rooms. For example, by placing closets in the master bathroom between the master bedroom and other rooms in a home creates a sound buffer zone which maximizes the privacy of the owners/parents.

Last are the hallways. Designers have mixed opinions concerning hallways, with some feeling they are wasted space and others believing they play an important role in transitioning between home zones. Personally, I feel hallways should be kept to a minimum. They cost just as much as the rest of the house to construct, yet provide little "livable area."

Considering the room classes and sizes discussed, a well designed three bedroom home may contain the following:

Dining Room	120 Sq. Ft.
Living Room	200 Sq. Ft.
Family Room	225 Sq. Ft.
Foyer	50 Sq. Ft.
Kitchen	100 Sq. Ft.
Master Bedroom	200 Sq. Ft.
Master Bathroom	100 Sq. Ft.
Bedroom	150 Sq. Ft.
Bedroom	150 Sq. Ft.
Guest Bathroom	75 Sq. Ft.
Master Bedroom Closet	75 Sq. Ft.
Bedroom and Linen Closets	40 Sq. Ft.
Hallways, Pantry, etc.	300 Sq. Ft.
Total	**1,785 Sq. Ft.**

As can be seen, a well designed three bedroom home may only contain 1,800 square feet of living area. (Garages are not included as living area). Therefore, you don't have to build or buy an enormous home for it to be comfortable and functional.

When thinking of floor plans, be sure to take into consideration the placement of furniture. In other words, how will furnishings fit into various rooms and the house as a whole. To visualize furniture placement, photocopy the floor plan and sketch in the furnishings you have or plan to buy once you move in. In this manner you can determine if the floor plan under consideration is actually livable.

How about bedrooms and fenestration (the orientation of windows in a room). Its best not to place a bed underneath a window due to drafts and the potential for harm resulting from storm damage, vandalism or intrusion. Does the door face directly into the bedroom, limiting privacy? These are factors you should consider when evaluating a floor plan.

If you are a growing family and plan to have more children, then you may want to consider buying/building a home which offers expansion opportunities. Specifically, don't buy a three bedroom home if you plan to have four or more children, for there will not be enough room for everybody. Such a situation will result in at least two children sharing a bedroom. While this is not so bad when the kids are young, it will most likely be a cause of constant friction when they reach adolescence and the privacy demanding teenage years. If proper planning is not implemented, short sightedness will cause you to sell a home in search of more space in the not-to-distant future.

One way to build expand-ability into a home yet keep costs to a minimum is to have a high roof line and "rough in" a bonus room over the garage or other living area. Just have a contractor install stairs in the garage and install adequate flooring supports to support future living area. Then, pre-wire electrical and HVAC duct service for an eventual second floor room. Over time, as your need for space increases, you can finish out this bonus room with carpet, padding, gypsum board walls and ceilings, etc.

As a final note on design, many architects and builders are searching for ways to make a home more friendly. In modern transient society, people are surrounded by strangers and nobody seems to know their neighbors. It's as if the competitive setting of the workplace has invaded our neighborhoods. To counter this trend, many developers are creating homes with features such as a large open porch on the front of the house to draw residents outside so they can see and visit with their neighbors.

The cold ugly face of garage doors are being moved from the front of the house to the side or rear, thus presenting a more inviting face and image. Streets are being lined with trees, sidewalks and streetlights. Neighborhoods are being developed with more parks, ponds and other recreational and aesthetic areas. These features can combine to create a more relaxed and enjoyable setting in which to live.

Summary
In summary, there are basically two types of housing available in the marketplace to meet the needs of home buyers; attached and detached. Attached units share a common wall, while detached units are stand alone structures. There are pros and cons to each. Attached units generally are less expensive due to smaller yards and shared walls, while detached homes are typically more expensive, but offer greater privacy and room for children to play.

There are some fundamental concepts associated with a well designed floor plan; including three distinct zones; adequate size and shape considerations; as well as friendly features and elevations. A home doesn't have to be large or fancy to flow well and feel comfortable.

6. HOME CONSTRUCTION

There are myriads of home construction characteristics and this text does not attempt to address all of them. However, a basic understanding of construction options is critical to a well informed home buying decision.

A home is constructed from the ground up, and this discussion follows the same path. I'll begin discussing house foundations; then move up to the walls, roof, and interior systems; and finally end up with the finishing touches.

Foundation

Homes are constructed on two types of foundations; on-grade and offgrade. An on-grade foundation is built directly on top of the ground and generally consists of a concrete slab poured at a thickness of 4 to 6 inches over a prepared homesite. The slab may or may not be anchored to the ground. If the homesite is relatively flat, then the foundation is typically not anchored, but just lays upon the ground. Such a foundation is called a "floating slab." If the homesite has an uneven terrain or the soil is prone to shifting, then the slab may be anchored to the ground via footings, which are holes dug into the ground and later filled with concrete. Footings serve to hold and anchor the slab in place.

Before an on-grade foundation is poured, the underlying site must be properly prepared. This includes leveling and compacting the soil so that it is firm enough to support the weight of the slab. Compaction specifications should be prepared by an architect or engineer after soil tests and construction plans have been completed.

After compaction, the soil is treated with pesticides to kill and prevent termites and other pests from entering the house from the ground-up. A vapor barrier consisting of a plastic tarp is then placed over the treated ground to separate moisture in the soil from the concrete slab which will be poured over top. If a vapor barrier is not installed, the concrete slab will drink up the moisture in the soil and be compromised.

Most on-grade slabs are reinforced with wire mesh rebar. Rebar typically consists of 10 millimeter wires woven into 6 inch squares, and is pulled up into the wet concrete once it is poured. Rebar serves to strengthen the foundation when the concrete dries. When rebar is used, it is important that all of the wire is completely covered with the concrete mixture. If any part is left exposed to air or water, then it may rust right through the entire slab.

Off-grade foundations are totally different. They are generally constructed at least 1.5 to 2.0 feet above the ground and consist of sub-flooring laid over footings or pilings. Sub-flooring typically consists of wood. The area created between the foundation and the ground is called the crawlspace. Offgrade foundations are often used on uneven or sloping sites, and on homesites subject to potential flooding, such as along waterways. The following is a photograph of a house with an off-grade foundation.

House With Off-Grade Foundation

There are pros and cons to both on-grade and off-grade foundations. Off-grade foundations generally have plumbing pipes in the crawlspace which are very accessible for service and repair. This is a pro. However, these accessible pipes are exposed to the effects of weather and may burst in freezing conditions; definitely a con. Off-grade foundations are more susceptible to termites, air intrusion, and the damaging effects of moisture.

In contrast, on-grade foundations insulate pipes from weather conditions by the concrete and underlying earth. They generally have a lower risk of bursting in inclimate weather, a definite pro. Also, a properly constructed on-grade foundation is much more resistant to termites, air intrusion, and moisture. However, if pipe problems do occur, they are very difficult to repair. Such repairs often require portions of the concrete foundation be torn up to get to the underlying pipes; an expensive con.

With either foundation, adequate site preparation is critical. This includes removing trees in the area where the home will be constructed, grading the site, possibly building up the home pad with sand or fill material, and applying pesticides to pre-treat the site against invasive and destructive bugs such as termites and carpenter ants.

If you love trees, be very careful during this process to save as many as possible, for trucks and other heavy equipment entering and exiting the construction site often injure root lines causing a slow death for trees which were meant to stay. The way to avoid this collateral damage is to mark the trees you want removed with a highly visible, florescent type tape. Then, construct a small barrier around the drip line of trees you want saved. Such barriers include small sticks placed around the drip line (the distance of branches from the trunk) connected with highly visible cloth or string.

To drive home your resolve to construction workers, include signs and place plywood in the area between the tree trunk and the stick line to soften the blow of any heavy materials. Also, include a small site diagram identifying your plan with the site contractor and have him sign off in agreement. As part of this agreement, include a fine of $500 per tree impact, regardless of severity. Don't allow the contractor to injure your trees and give you the standard line that the tree will be unaffected. Such injuries are usually fatal, but may take 5 years to be realized.

Once marked trees are removed from the construction area, the site can be cleared and graded level. If the home pad is in a low lying area of the site, be sure to import fill material and buildup the foundation to elevate it from water which may collect during periods of heavy rain. Ideally, the home pad should be developed on the highest point of the site to ensure water drains away, not toward, the home.

The last step before construction of the foundation is treating it with pesticides. Unfortunately, many companies do not apply the proper amount or type of chemical. As a result, many newly developed homes have bug problems. This is a serious problem, for undetected bug invasion can destroy the structural integrity of a home.

The misapplication of pesticides is a tough problem to police and local building inspectors are too few to be present at every site pretreatment. Many states recognizes this situation is a severe threat to the economic health of its citizens and have responded by making available university based entomologists (bug scientists) to oversee site pretreatment and ensure proper chemicals and application. This is generally a free or low cost service available to consumers. It is my recommendation anyone building a new home should take advantage of such free expertise if available by contacting nearby university entomology departments

Frame
Once the foundation is constructed, the next step is to build the frame of the home. The frame is generally constructed over, and on top of, the foundation. In residential construction, framing is typically masonry or wood. However, steel framing is becoming popular, and if costs remain low it will probably be the framing choice of the future.

In masonry construction, concrete blocks and brick are the fundamental building materials. These are most often prefabricated at the factory and come in standard sizes. Walls are constructed by stacking blocks or bricks and securing them together through the use of rebar and mortar. As previously discussed, rebar consists of steel wire used to strengthen a masonry area. Mortar is the cement (glue) used to hold the blocks together.

Concrete is a mixture of cement, water and aggregates, which when mixed properly and hardened makes a very durable and strong building material. It is formed by combining the appropriate proportions of cement and water, and then adding aggregates. The aggregates are stirred into the mixture until thoroughly coated with the moistened cement. Then, after the cement dries and hardens, it binds all the aggregates tightly together to form concrete.

People sometimes confuse concrete and cement. Concrete is the final product, and cement is the glue-like material used to bind together aggregates. Aggregates which are most often used in home construction include sand, crushed stone, coquina (shells), and small rocks.

Initially, concrete block construction was used solely for structural support purposes and was painted or covered over with another form of veneer such as brick or stucco. Today, however, concrete blocks come in several architectural styles which can make an appealing exterior finish.

Other masonry building materials used in home construction include brick and stone. Brick is a clay product which is hardened in kilns under extremely high temperatures, and stone such as granite and marble are quarried from the earth in buildable sizes and shapes. Like concrete, brick and stone are set in place with mortar.

The advantages of masonry building materials are they don't rot or warp, and they are very low maintenance materials. In addition, they are impervious to fungi and insect invasion. The disadvantages are masonry materials are stiff and may develop cracks over time as a result of settling and erosion. Also, they are poor insulators and are the most expensive form of framing.

When built, masonry walls should include control and expansion joints to relieve stresses caused by foundation settlement, earth movement, and changes in temperature. These joints are like specially designed cracks which serve as shock absorbers and allow a wall to contract and expand without crumbling. In addition, they should include weep holes at the base of the exterior walls near the foundation to drain out moisture.

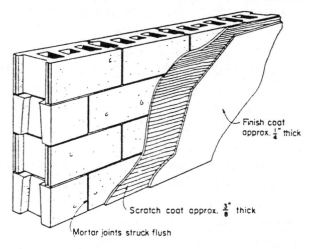

Finish coat approx. $\frac{1}{4}$" thick

Scratch coat approx. $\frac{3}{8}$" thick

Mortar joints struck flush

Diagram of concrete block framing

Wood is the other primary framing material used in residential construction. Wood framing typically consists of sawed boards four-to-six inches deep and two-to-four inches wide, thus the terms "two-by-four" and "two-by-six." These "studs" come in eight-to-twelve foot lengths to correspond with the ceiling height of most homes. In construction, they are nailed directly to the foundation and are normally spaced at 16 to 24 inch intervals.

Once the wood frame exterior walls are in place, an exterior sheathing is added for strength. Sheathing generally consists of plywood, pressboard, or insulation board and serves to link all the studs together, as well as provide a barrier to moisture. Solid plywood is the most expensive form of sheathing. Pressboard, also known as OSB, is made of small wood chips glued together and is less expensive and more common. Once the sheathing is in-place, the exterior siding may be installed. Common sidings include brick, wood planks, wood shakes, stucco, and textured plywood.

Many types of softwoods and hardwoods are used in home construction. Softwoods include species such as Pine, Fir, Spruce, and Cedar, and these woods are often used in framing and flooring. Hardwoods include species such as Oak, Cherry, Mahogany, and Hickory, and these are often used in trim, staircase and furniture construction.

The advantages of wood are it is more flexible than masonry products and it can absorb a higher degree of settlement without cracking. It is also typically a few dollars per square foot cheaper. The disadvantages are wood can rot, warp, burn, and be damaged by fungi and insect invasion. Therefore, while wood frame homes are more flexible than masonry homes, they are more maintenance intensive as well.

Wood should be treated and dried before construction to provide extra strength against moisture, fungi, and insects, and it should always be protected against wetness and damaging organisms. Therefore, if you build a wood frame home, make sure the wood does not get soaked during construction and keep it a safe distance from the ground to separate it from moisture, fungi and insects. Also, have a pest control service pretreat the homesite with termite and organism killers before construction and then annually retreat the home to protect against these problems later. Skimping in this area can have devastating consequences. The following are a diagram and photograph of wood frame construction with plywood sheathing.

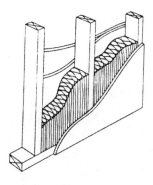

Diagram

Wood Frame Construction

One way many home buyers can combine the flexibility of wood framing with the strength and durability of masonry materials is to build the frame of the home with wood products, and then apply an exterior veneer of masonry materials such as brick or stucco. In this way, the exterior presented to the weather is of the most durable building materials available, yet the structural frame remains maximally flexible and inexpensive. The following is a picture of this type of construction.

Combination Masonry and Frame Construction

Steel framing is gaining popularity due to the falling cost of steel and new designs which use thin but strong studs. Light weight concrete panels, insulation board or plywood can be used as the exterior sheathing material, and any form of exterior veneer can be applied. The benefits of steel framing are its strength and durability. A galvanized coating protects from rust, and it won't rot, burn or get eaten by bugs. Yet, it is flexible. It is superior to concrete block framing, for it can expand and contract with changes in temperature without cracking or crumbling over time, and it doesn't require a wood framed roof (which most masonry homes include).

The primary concern with steel framing is the heat/cold transfer of metal. Specifically, steel studs are conductors, not insulators, and can absorb outside heat or cold and radiate it into the home. This is termed the "thermal bridge" effect. One way of eliminating this problem is to place adequately sized insulation board between the studs and the exterior veneer. The insulation board vastly reduces the bridge radiating effect. The following is a picture and diagram of steel frame construction:

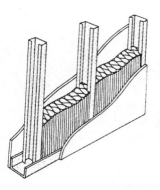

Diagram

Steel Frame Construction

Wall Veneers

The most common veneers used in home construction include brick, coquina, stucco, wood siding, and plywood. Masonry veneers are the lowest maintenance but the most expensive to install, while wood veneers are the least expensive but the most maintenance intensive. The following series of pictures illustrates various exterior coverings.

Brick Veneer Home

Coquina Veneer Home

Stucco Veneer Home

Wood Siding Veneer

Plywood Veneer

With brick veneer, the frame and support of the house is usually made of concrete block, wood or steel. The brick, in this case, is a "curtain wall" serving only as a durable, low maintenance surface of the home. Such a wall has no structural function. In contrast, a "Norwegian Brick" home has brick as both the framing and exterior facing material.

Stucco is a cementuous product which can be applied over masonry, wood or steel framing. In the case of masonry framing, the stucco is applied directly over the block. However, in wood and steel framing a surface must be created to which the stucco can adhere. As such, a lath (metal wire panel) is attached to the exterior sheathing and the stucco is applied to the lathe. Stucco is generally applied in three coats; scratch coat (1st), brown coat (2nd), and finish coat (3rd). Most stucco applications range in thickness from 3/8 to 5/8 inches.

There have been several advances in stucco applications, making this form of veneer increasingly popular due to its relatively low cost. Pigments can be added so that painting is never required, only periodic washing. Insulating and water repellant materials can be added to enhance the stucco's strength against outside elements. In addition, stucco can be worked to create various effects and designs on a home which are not possible with other veneers. Detailed information on stucco and concrete block construction can be obtained from the Portland Cement Association headquartered in Skokie, Illinois. The phone number is (800) 868-6733.

In wood siding, boards are lapped over each other and nailed to the frame. This lap method helps reduce the damaging effects of moisture. With plywood siding, large sheets are nailed to the frame. Both forms should be carefully caulked and painted to minimize the effects of water and insect intrusion.

Roof

In residential construction, the roof is typically constructed of wood or metal studs tied down to the load bearing exterior walls. The most common form of roof framing is the truss, which is a prefabricated triangular shaped wood product. Trusses are installed in a series; like dominos. Over this roof frame is placed an exterior sheathing material such as plywood, pressboard, insulation board or lightweight concrete panels. The sheathing is then covered with a vapor barrier such as tar or asphalt paper, and finally the veneer is applied; such as shingles, metal panels, tile, etc.

Roof designs vary, from high pitched hip roofs to relatively flat roofs. The type selected should be a function of climate and desired aesthetics. For example, in the Southeast, where it is hot and rains a lot, high pitched roofs are preferred. The pitch facilitates the drainage of rain water and, since hot air rises, keeps the heat in the attic far away from the living area. In cold arid climates which experience little precipitation, the opposite may be preferred. A low pitch roof design keeps the heat closer to the living area. However, for Northern climates which experience a large amount of snowfall, then a high pitch may be necessary to keep the snow from piling up and crushing the roof frame due to extreme weight. The following series of illustrations depict various roof styles:

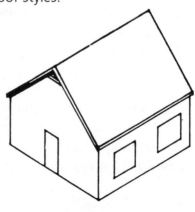

Gable Roof

GABLE

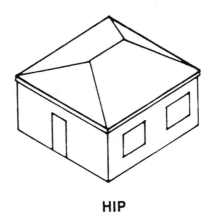

HIP

Hip Roof

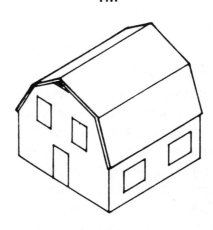

GAMBREL

Gambrel Roof

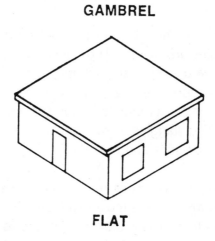

FLAT

Flat Roof

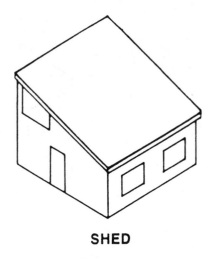

Shed Roof   **SHED**

Roof Veneers

Roof veneers include materials such as composite shingles, wood shakes, ceramic tiles, and metal panels. The purpose of all roof veneers is to protect the plywood sheathing and wood framing underneath, as well as the entire interior of the home from water, moisture and the elements. Therefore, all roof coverings should be constructed of water resistant materials and roof lines should expedite the removal of water. If water sits on a roof and doesn't drain, it will eventually cause damage to a home.

By far, the most often used roof covering consists of shingles. Shingles are made of fiberglass, asphalt, and other materials, and are placed in an overlapping fashion from the eave to the highest roof line. They come in sheets which are relatively easy, but time consuming, to install. The main thing to consider when choosing shingles is their quality. Shingles are rated by life expectancy, style and content.

Metal panels and ceramic barrel tile are the longest lasting roof coverings, and the most expensive. Generally, they are installed to create a specific look as opposed to solely extending the life of the roof cover. For example, metal roofs are often used in

"Low Country" and "Key West Cracker" style designs, while barrel tile gives a definite Mediterranean effect.

All home buyers should recognize that roof coverings, no matter what type, are temporary and will require periodic repairs and replacement over time. Even the best quality roof veneers typically last no more than 25 to 30 years. The following pictures illustrate various roof coverings:

Shingle Roof Covering

Wood Shake Roof Covering

Metal Roof Covering

Ceramic Tile

Insulation

After the exterior walls and roof are framed, insulation should be installed to protect the interior living space from outside temperature conditions. Bat and blown insulation are best suited for frame walls (wood or steel) where there are gaps between studs which can be filled. In contrast, rigid insulation (board type) is best suited for masonry walls where there is little space available to fill.

The type of insulation applied is a function of the climate and type of home construction involved. To optimize your investment, consult with local utility company representatives and gather their cost-benefit analysis results of insulation applications in the area. There is a point at which more insulation is not cost effective, for the reduction in energy costs is less than the cost of the insulation. Utility companies can typically tell you the optimum amount and type of insulation to be installed.

The interior walls of a home are typically not insulated, either thermally or acoustically. Rather, only exterior and ceiling walls are insulated, for these are the barriers separating the interior living space from the climate and moisture outside. However, additional insulation in certain interior walls may be beneficial. For example, sound insulation placed into walls is beneficial if bedrooms are located near family and dining rooms, or if the parent's master bedroom is near the children's rooms.

Doors and Windows

There are basically two types of doors in every house; exterior and interior. Exterior doors face the outside of the home and must be resilient against the effects of weather and the wiles of criminals. As such, they are usually made of solid wood, metal panels, or a combination thereof. Interior doors, on the other hand, are only used as visual and sound barriers, and they are not exposed to the outside elements. Therefore, they are typically less hardy and often consist of hollow core wood construction. The primary exceptions are doors to the master bedroom or study, where a solid core door is often used as a sound insulating device.

Windows serve three basic functions;

　　　　1) interior illumination

　　　　2) exterior view

　　　　3) ventilation

Not all windows provide all three functions. For example, a fixed pane window may provide illumination and a view, but it cannot be opened to provide ventilation. Likewise, an opaque window in a bathroom may provide illumination and ventilation, but it does not provide a view. There are many different styles and designs of windows, but the most common found in residential construction are fixed pane, hung, sliding, awning, casement, pivot, and jalousie.

Interior Walls

Interior walls and ceilings are generally constructed of wood or metal framing and are less sturdy than exterior framing, since they are generally not load bearing. The majority of interior walls are constructed of wood, but some of the better quality homes are now installing metal framing, which until recently was reserved for commercial buildings. Both wood and metal are good framing materials for they are lightweight, relatively inexpensive, flexible and durable. Metal framing is superior, however, since it is not susceptible to moisture or insect invasion and has no tendency to rot, warp or decay. In addition, it is not combustible.

In the past, interior framed walls were covered with plaster applied over a metal lath. Today, the vast majority of interior walls are covered with sheets of gypsum board, also known as sheet rock. Gypsum board has become the covering of choice because it comes in standardized sheets, is relatively inexpensive and easy to work with, and it presents a clean uniform finish after installation. In addition, it is not as susceptible to cracking and crumbling as plaster.

Gypsum board consists of a plaster-like material covered on both sides by a paper backing. The paper serves two functions. One, it provides extra support to prevent crumbling of the plaster-like material inside, and, two, it presents a smooth even finish for painting or wall papering. Gypsum board comes in pre-cut sizes which can be easily tailored on-site with a razor knife during construction. The boards are nailed or screwed into studs. Seems and nail holes are then filled with tape and putty and sanded smooth.

The most common wall covering is paint. For interior purposes, the paints of choice are typically flat or semigloss for walls in the bedrooms, hallways, den, dining room, and living room. Semigloss and gloss are usually used on wood trim, and in areas such as the kitchen, laundry room, and bathroom. However, semigloss paint is becoming a popular wall covering for every room, especially in houses with children, for this paint surface often allows dirt and food marks to be wiped clean with a damp cloth.

When evaluating paints, make sure the one you choose does not contain lead. Lead based paints are no longer available on the market, but some older homes still have lead based paint on the walls. Lead is a proven health hazard and should be avoided.

Other wall coverings include wallpaper and wood paneling. Wallpaper is a paper, cloth or vinyl based product with a decorative illustration or relief. Wallpaper comes in two basic types; pre-glued and plain. With the latter, glue must be added.

An important point to consider with wallpaper is its proper application varies depending on the climate. One problem with wallpaper is it can become a vapor barrier when installed on a wall. As such, when placed on an exterior wall it will prevent moisture transfer. This is not necessarily good, for in humid climates wallpaper can cause moisture to build up inside the exterior wall cavity, eventually causing mildew, mold, and rot.

An article written by Gary Cook and Virginia Peart published in the November 1993 issue of Today's Air Conditioning, reports "vapor barriers...should never be used on the inside of exterior walls. This includes vinyl wall coverings." The application of border (a thin strip of wallpaper along the ceiling line) is probably not much of a concern for significant wall function is not affected.

Floors

The most common floor coverings in residential construction include carpet, wood, ceramic, and vinyl tile. Floor coverings not only make attractive finishes, but they also serve as insulation and provide cushion over the hard foundational sub-floor.

By far the most common floor covering in modern construction is carpeting. This type became popular during the past fifty years. Previously, carpeting was made of wool and the manufacturing process was labor intensive, thus making the end product expensive. As a result, only the well-to-do had carpeting in their homes. In addition, carpet was difficult to properly clean and maintain prior to the invention of the electric vacuum cleaner.

Today, however, with advances in manufacturing technology; the advent of new fibers such as rayon, nylon, and polyesters; and the low-cost proliferation of vacuum cleaners, carpet has become affordable and practical. It is currently one of the least expensive and most popular types of floor covering. Some of the advantages of carpet are it is the floor covering standard in moderate and middle income housing; it is relatively inexpensive; and it is pleasant to walk on due to its cushion and insulating characteristics. In addition, it comes in a variety of colors, patterns, and weaves.

Some of the disadvantages of carpet are: no matter how good your vacuum cleaner is, carpet remains difficult to "deep clean"; it can stain and tear; and it loses resiliency over time. Due these detractions, the average life of good quality carpet ranges from only five to seven years, afterwhich replacement is recommended.

Most mass produced carpet is tufted, which means thousands of strands of material are embedded into a base. According to the Carpet and Rug Institute (based in Dalton, Georgia), nearly 97% of all carpets manufactured today have tufts made of synthetic fibers such as nylon, olefin, polyester. or acrylic. Few are made of natural materials such as wool.

There are two basic types of carpet; loop (Berber) and cut (shag) pile. The Carpet and Rug Institute recommends loop pile carpeting in high traffic areas such as family rooms and hallways due its high resiliency and long life. In low traffic, more luxurious areas such as dining rooms and living rooms, they recommend cut pile carpeting. It all depends on the effect and life expectancy you desire. More information in this regard can be obtained from CRI at 1-800-882-8846.

Carpet should be installed with good quality padding. Padding not only provides cushion, but also prolongs the life of carpet by reducing wear and maintaining resiliency. The Independent Textile Testing Service studied the effects of cushion on carpet life and discovered the following:

> "...a test was used whereby different carpet/cushion systems were subjected to rolling a chair with a 150 lb. weight over them 20,000 times. The results indicate that carpets with no cushion had an average 19.3% loss in pile height as opposed to a 5% to 10% loss in thickness for carpets with a separate cushion."

Therefore, good padding is generally a wise investment. However, to optimize your investment, the cost of padding should be less than the anticipated loss in carpet life over time as a result of not including padding.

According to the Carpet Cushion Council of Riverside Connecticut, there are three basic types of cushion; urethane, fiber, and rubber. The thickness of the padding is a function of the type being laid and its traffic pattern. The Council recommends that ribbed rubber cushion have a thickness of 0.285 inches in light traffic areas such as the living room, dining room, and bedrooms. However, they recommend a larger thickness of 0.330 inches in heavy duty traffic areas such as family rooms, hallways, and staircases. Don't just assume more thickness is better. For example, with densified prime urethane cushion, the recommended thickness actually decreases in high traffic areas. In all cases, however, the Council discourages the application of any cushion greater than 0.5 inches of thickness. A brochure detailing the exact recommendation of thickness by cushion type can be obtained free of charge by calling the Carpet Cushion Institute at (203) 637-1312.

Most medical experts agree that carpet should be avoided if a family member suffers from allergies or asthma. The problem is, carpet is difficult to keep "deep clean." As a result, it tends to collect dust and particulates over time. Such dust buildup is a feasting and breeding ground for mites; small almost microscopic bugs, which are a severe allergen to many people. In addition, carpet padding may become damp against the sub-floor and produce molds and mildew. Therefore, if an allergy or asthma sufferer is in the family, it is probably best to install a different type of floor covering than carpet. However, if alternatives are not affordable and carpeting is used, don't glue it to the foundational sub-floor so it can be easily replaced; treat the carpet with a dust mite killer recommended by an asthma and allergy expert; and invest in the best vacuum cleaner you can afford. Probably the best measure of defense is a well functioning air conditioning system which keeps inside humidity levels low. Dust mites can't live in a low humidity environment.

Other popular and relatively inexpensive forms of floor coverings are vinyl tile and linoleum. These synthetic materials come in sheets and are glued to the foundational sub-floor. They are not as comfortable to walk on as carpet, but they are much softer than wood or ceramic tile.

Most average-to-lower quality homes have vinyl tile or linoleum in the kitchen and bathroom, where ceramic tile would be found in higher quality homes. The advantages of vinyl tile and linoleum are they are inexpensive, easy to install, and they come in a variety of colors and patterns. The disadvantages are they can be scuffed and torn rather easily. Most such floors have a life similar to that of carpet, ranging from seven to ten years, afterwhich it is recommended they be replaced.

Wood floors are making a comeback in the market due their natural beauty, ease of maintenance and long term durability. Wood floors can be installed in a variety of colors and patterns, and thus are a very flexible material from a design standpoint. They can be installed in both on-grade and off-grade construction. If used in conjunction with an on-grade foundation, the slab is generally recessed to allow for the thickness of the wood.

On-grade wood floors tend to be quieter to walk on than off-grade floors since the concrete slab acts as a sound insulator and because there is no baffle zone created by the crawlspace. In contrast, off-grade wood floors are noisy to walk on, but give a home the "historic" feel, which many find charming.

Wood floors generally come in three types; strip, plank and parquet. Strips consist of long thin pieces of wood; planks are long flat boards; and parquet consists of small wood tiles and blocks. Today, such floors can be installed two ways; either glued down or nailed down. Glue down floors are typically a laminated product which comes in sheets approximately 1/2" to 3/4" thick and are glued directly to the foundational sub-floor. In contrast, nail-down floors come in the same or greater thickness, but are nailed directly onto plywood sub-flooring.

Properly installed and finished wood floors are a strong and easy to maintain floor covering. Periodically, depending on wear, they should be refinished by a professional. Such refinishing involves removing the old finish, re-sanding the wood surface, and applying a new finish coat. If properly maintained, wood floors can last the life of a home.

One note regarding wood floors. In nail down floors, I recommend the wood planks and strips be nailed into good quality exterior grade solid plywood as opposed to press board plywood. The problem with press board is it typically contains formaldehyde, which emits gasses over time and is an allergen to many people. Therefore, press board should be avoided, even though solid wood costs more money. As in most building materials, spending a little more on quality can make a big difference.

Ceramic tile is a popular floor covering. Ceramic tile is a masonry product installed in a bed of mortar. Expansion joints are placed between tiles, and these joints allow the tile to expand and contract in temperature changes without cracking. These expansion joints are filled with decorative mortar and also help keep the tile firmly in place. The advantages of ceramic tile are, it is a very durable covering which is easy to maintain. In addition, tiles don't rot and are impervious to fungi and insects. The disadvantages are, tile is an extremely hard and unforgiving surface, and it can develop cracks and chips over time.

Cost wise, good quality carpeting will generally run from $2.50 to $3.00 per square foot, including installation (though it is usually sold by the square yard); vinyl and linoleum tile will typically run from $3.00 to $4.00 per square foot, including installation; ceramic tile typically runs from $4.00 to $10.00 per square foot depending on size and style, including installation; and wood floors will typically run from $8.00 to $10.00 per square foot, including installation. As can be seen, tile and wood floors are the most expensive, but last the longest, whereas carpet, vinyl and linoleum are the least expensive, but require replacement every five to seven years, depending on wear.

Electrical Systems

Modern homes with heavy electrical equipment such as ovens, water heaters, clothes dryers, and air conditioning systems typically have a 120/230 volt, 200-400 ampere single phase three wire electrical system. The three prong system includes a neutral grounded wire and two hot wires. Wiring is installed inside the walls of a house with receptacles placed to access the electricity and the system is generally laid via conduits (tubes) connecting with the fuse box. The fuse box is like a distribution facility; electricity comes from an outside line to the fuse box and is then distributed via the various conduits to all areas of the home.

Most residential electrical conduits consist of a plastic type piping. However, high quality residential and most commercial construction use metal conduit. I recommend metal, for if you ever have electrical problems, wires can be pulled and run through metal conduit to fix the problem. Such repairs are not always possible with plastic conduit.

Older homes without modern fixtures are often equipped with less voltage and amperes than current homes and may only have a two wire system. Such homes may be unable to handle the installation of modern equipment in a planned renovation, unless the entire electrical system is upgraded. Therefore, before you plan to buy an older home and renovate it, make sure you examine its electrical system.

You can discover the type of system in a home by reading the fuse box and examining the electrical outlets. The inside panel of the fuse box should report its voltage and ampere capacity, and a two prong outlet indicates a two wire system; currently obsolete.

Plumbing Systems

Plumbing systems are somewhat similar to electrical systems.

Service comes into the house from a central line, either a public line or well line, and then water is distributed throughout the house via various pipes. Water generally comes into the house from underneath the ground. To go uphill like this, it is pressurized.

In a community water system, homes in an area are connected to a centralized water plant which has access to a water source, such as a river, lake, or aquifer. The water obtained from this source is then treated with chemicals such as chlorine to kill bacteria and other organisms to make the water safe for drinking and household use. The treated water is then stored and later distributed to homes via a pressurized water main system. The water main connects with small pipes leading to houses, and these pipes have meters to monitor water usage for billing purposes.

The other primary source of water is a private well system. Wells can either be deep or shallow depending on the depth and quality of the underlying water source. Well water is typically piped directly into the house untreated. This type of water service has no monthly base or usage charge and the only expenses are associated with pump and pipe maintenance and electricity. In general, community water service is preferred over well service because the quality of the water can be monitored and managed by trained professionals, even though it costs more.

Before buying a home, it is a good idea to have the water tested by a local environmental firm. Tests are relatively inexpensive (usually less than $100) and can identify problems with the water, such as any residues or chemicals which may be present. Such tests should be performed by an independent lab, and not a company which sells water softeners or other water treatment products. The opinions of the latter may be biased.

Water samples should be taken early in the morning after about eight hours of non-use of house plumbing systems. In addition, samples should be taken from two sources, i.e. the kitchen faucet and the bathroom faucet. This allows any deposits which may build up in the pipes to be tested as well. Tests indicating high levels of bacteria, pesticides, or lead are a good warning not to buy the home.

The two primary types of sewer service include community systems and septic tanks. Community sewer service operates much like community water service, except in the opposite manner. Whereas water systems pipe water from a central treatment facility to the home, sewer systems pipe sewage and waste from the home to a central treatment facility. Sewer lines are not pressurized like water lines, rather they typically operate via gravity flow. If the lines extend a long distance to the treatment facility, then lift stations are required along the way to pipe the sewage up to a high point from which it can again use gravity to flow to the treatment facility. Most large public sewer facilities are government owned and operated.

Septic tanks are used in areas where public systems are not available, such as in rural and semi-rural locations. In a septic system, the sewage and waste water from a home flow down through pipes via gravity pull to an underground storage tank, which is usually constructed of concrete. In this tank, bacteria breaks down the sewage. Then, liquid residues flow through holes in the tank to an adjoining drain field and percolate down through the soil.

If the water table is high on a site, then septic tanks cannot be buried underground, for the underlying water table will push the tank back up through the ground like a fishing bobber under water. In such cases, above ground tanks are required. These tanks are constructed in what appears to be a mound in the yard. A pump is installed to pump the sewage up into the tank because gravity flow cannot work in such cases.

In general, like water systems, community sewer systems are preferred over septic tank systems when possible, primarily because the waste and its treatment can be moved off-site away from your home. In addition, septic tanks are maintenance intensive and must be pumped periodically. An overflowing septic tank can back up into a home making a smelly, nasty mess. If a well and septic system are jointly used on a site, it is important that the well be located as far as possible from the septic tank in an attempt to keep wastes from percolating down to the home's water source.

Water heaters are simple plumbing devices consisting of a water storage tank, heating elements, thermostats and insulation. When cold water comes into the tank the thermostat detects a loss in temperature and activates the heating elements. The system is designed to keep "hot" water stored at a fairly constant temperature, generally 120 to 140 degrees Fahrenheit.

The water heater should be a full size tank (40 to 60 gallons), otherwise the home may run out of hot water after every shower or dishwasher cycle. It should be well insulated to prevent heat loss. A poorly insulated water heater will cause the heating coils to operate more often, thus increasing energy costs and reducing the life of the coils. Due to possible fire and explosion risks, water heaters should be placed in the service zone of a home, such as the garage or utility room, and away from the social and private zones.

When dealing with plumbing fixtures, don't skimp on quality. Poor quality fixtures will cause problems and necessitate replacement, thus costing more in the long run. For example, poor quality faucets tend to leak, poor quality tubs tend to rust or develop spongy bottoms, and poor quality toilets tend to run continuously and develop seat separation. Good quality (but not necessarily the top of the line) plumbing fixtures should help reduce future troubles. Ideas to keep in mind include single mold enamel coated or fiberglass shower/tub enclosures (easy to clean and maintain), washerless faucets, and cast iron tubs with a good acid resistant enamel finish.

HVAC System

The last major home system is the heating, ventilation, and air conditioning (HVAC) system. This system is used to control temperature and humidity within a home. There are various types of systems in use and this section will discuss a few.

All types of heating systems work on the same basic principle. Energy in fuel is transformed into heat, which in turn is used to warm the inside of a home. The primary difference in systems, therefore, relates to the source of heat and its form of distribution. The two primary sources of heat in homes are combustion and resistance.

In combustion heat, fuels are converted into heat through burning. The most common combustion fuels are oil and natural gas. The ignition source is a flame called a pilot light which ignites the fuel, converting it into heat. Since a fire is involved, combustible systems produce on-site emissions. The smoke and odor is typically minimal in a well designed and properly operated system. However, malfunctions can be deadly. As a result, a smart home with a combustion heating system includes CO (carbon monoxide) detectors, which alert occupants to high levels of the deadly odorless by-product of burning combustion fuels.

The other primary type involves resistance heat, with the energy source being electricity. In these systems, a resistor transforms electricity into heat. Electric systems do not involve combustion and thus produce no on-site emissions. Though electricity is cleaner, it is often more expensive and less reliable than combustible fuel sources.

Once heat is generated, it is distributed in one of two primary ways; a central or room system. In a central system, heat is distributed throughout all rooms in a home via ductwork. In the case of air systems, which are the most popular type of central system, a fan blows heated air through pipes called ducts into the various rooms. A return duct then sucks the air back into the system to the heat source, and the process starts all over again. A thermostat controls the fan and heat source to maintain a fairly constant temperature throughout the home.

In contrast, a room system serves only one room. Examples of a room system include a wall or window mounted unit, a kerosene space heater, a woodstove or a fireplace. Room systems are limited in their heating and cooling capability, and are usually found in older homes lacking central systems. Often, they are used as supplements or in emergencies.

Air conditioning systems work on the same principle. Air is forced over a series of cooling coils and then distributed through the house. Warm air is then sucked into return ducts and the cooling process begins again.

There are some key points to consider when evaluating a HVAC system, for this is a very important part of the house. Most air conditioning professionals recommend that an HVAC system have the capacity to recirculate the air in a home at a rate of about four times per hour, and that a relative humidity level of approximately 50% be maintained. Therefore, movement, and not just temperature, is important. Have an air conditioning engineer assess the appropriate size unit for the home you are building or buying.

When installing the HVAC system, exterior mounted equipment should be placed well away from obstructions so that air can move freely over coils. Air handlers should be placed away from sources of pollution such as garbage cans, septic tanks, garages, and bathroom vents. This prevents pollution from being sucked into the house if a duct leak occurs. Also, special filters which charge and trap dust (electrostatic filters) should be considered to reduce indoor pollutants. However, such filters should include collectors, or the ionized dust particles will cling to furniture and walls creating a haze over time. It is also a good idea to install a heat recovery ventilator in your HVAC system. Such a device increases the amount of fresh air taken into a home, yet does not create a significant loss of system efficiency (heat or cold loss). See a professional for details and proper sizing.

To promote efficiency, HVAC ducts should run along the middle of the house away from the outside walls, which are sources of hot and cold transfer in a home. Vents should be aimed toward the exterior walls, washing them with conditioned air to cut down on energy transfer. Ducts should be cleaned every five years or so by an air conditioning service to remove dust, bacteria, and mold.

Lastly, most old air conditioning systems use Freon as the coolant. Unfortunately, Freon emits CFCs (chlorofluorocarbons) which have been shown to reduce ozone; a protective atmospheric screen that reduces the damaging rays of the sun. As a result, the United States is part of a worldwide agreement to reduce and eventually eliminate CFC use. Therefore, existing Freon powered air conditioning units will eventually have to either be replaced, converted to use the new non-CFC coolants, or the owner will have to pay skyrocketing prices for the limited supply of Freon reserves. All are costly alternatives. Therefore, home buyers should recognize the Freon crisis and take steps to protect themselves.

Lighting Systems
Lighting is usually a matter of preference, with the exception of some basic rules. Special attention should be given the lighting in the kitchen, bathroom, and the dining rooms.

I believe kitchens should be well lit. This is a work area of the house, and, as such, good lighting is essential. To achieve this result, many designers use fluorescent strip bulbs recessed into the ceiling. Such bulbs tend to wash an area with light and special reflectors placed in the ceiling can enhance this effect.

The dining room should also be well lit. However, in this room, fluorescent lighting is too impersonal and overpowering. Instead, an intimate and social atmosphere is desired. Therefore, most designers use chandeliers equipped with candle shaped bulbs and dimming switches to achieve this effect.

Lastly, the bathroom should be well lit for grooming and health maintenance purposes. Most designers recommend either fluorescent fixtures or incandescent strip mounted bulb fixtures. The latter is generally preferred, for it gives the best natural color to skin, while fluorescent lighting tends to wash out color. Also, a radiant heat lamp is a good idea for the bathroom, especially as a source of supplemental heat during winter months.

Lighting in other rooms of the house can generally be satisfied through lamps and ceiling fixtures. One popular trend is to have ceiling fans equipped with a light kit.

Security Systems

Other systems often found in modern homes include security and computer systems. As a result of rising crime and associated fears, more and more families are installing security systems in their homes. Such systems are generally a deterrent against unskilled burglars and juvenile delinquents. However, few security systems are a match for highly skilled professional burglars.

A home security system can have several different types of sensors. Entry and breakage sensors are typically placed at access points such as windows and doors, while motion detectors can be placed both in and outside the home to detect movement. Some upscale homes have lazer trip wires, thermal sensors, and video cameras as well. The typical security system comes equipped with a battery to provide system power for one to two days in case electric service is cut.

In addition to hardware, there are several forms of response. Basic systems have only an alarm when activated, such as a loud ringing bell. Other more sophisticated systems include an alarm and off-site professional monitoring. When tripped, the alarm notifies the off-site monitoring personnel, who then call the home. If the proper password is not given, police are dispatched to investigate. The intricacy of the system should be a function of a family's security needs. In general, a system with entry, glass break and motion detection is sufficient for the average middle class family.

Security systems can also be equipped with fire, smoke and medical alarms. The fire and smoke alarms not only alert residents, but send a message to local monitors and fire stations. Medical alarms are helpful for elderly and ill residents, for they can contact emergency squads with the push of a button.

In addition to electronic systems, good home design and foresight can reduce crime potential. For example, installing dead bolts and peep holes in exterior doors, lighting which illuminates the exterior of the home, and keeping shrubbery clipped low to eliminate hiding places are all preventive measures a homeowner can take to reduce the threat of crime. For more good thoughts on home security, contact your local police for a home evaluation.

Home Office Systems

In this world of computers, fax machines, modems, and telecommuting, the home office is becoming ever more popular. In fact, some studies predict that 25% of the work force will be working at home by the early 2000s. While this is hard to imagine today, many homebuilders are trying to capture this growing market by equipping homes with workstations. Typical improvements include an in-house office with separate phone lines for fax machines and modems, and built-in desks and cabinetry. If you plan to work at home on a full or part time basis, then consider these features before buying or building.

Landscaping

Landscaping is the finishing touch to a good quality home; it's the icing on the cake. Type and quantity should be a function of climate, soil conditions, and budgetary constraints.

For example, a well landscaped homesite in the Southeast will typically have a grassed yard along with extensive shrubbery, flowers, and trees. The ample rain in the region provides most of the required irrigation, but a sprinkler system is usually installed as a supplemental source during periods of drought. In contrast, a well landscaped lot in the arid Southwest may have a rock or gravel yard interlaced with cacti and other plants which require little water maintenance due to the lack of precipitation and the high cost of water.

If possible, hire a landscape architect. At a minimum, get advice from a reputable landscape contractor. As with anything associated with your home, paying a little extra to do it right the first time will save/earn you money in the long run.

Summary

There are numerous construction combinations available in the marketplace and a smart buyer should be aware of options. Foundations may be on-grade or offgrade; framing may be masonry, wood, or steel; veneers may be brick, stone, stucco, wood siding, wood shakes, or plywood; roof veneers may be fiberglass shingles, wood shakes, ceramic tile, or metal; insulation may be loose-fill, flexible, blown, or rigid; doors may be solid, hollow core, or metal reinforced; windows can provide illumination, view, and ventilation, or a combination thereof; interior wall framing may be of wood or metal; floor coverings may be carpet, vinyl, wood, and tile; etc. All such features have pros and cons. Potential home buyers should choose the construction options which best meet the design characteristics of the home they seek and are conducive to the climate of the area, as well as being within budgetary constraints.

7. EVALUATING A USED HOME

If you are considering the purchase of an existing home, there are several items to carefully evaluate. The most important are the effects and presence of depreciation. Basically, depreciation is a loss in value resulting from any cause, and there are three basic types; physical, functional, and external. These items will cost you money, so screen for them carefully.

Physical Depreciation

Physical depreciation is a loss in the value of a home resulting from a deterioration in the physical condition of the improvements. Note; the homesite does not deteriorate, only the building. The loss in value may be a result of deferred maintenance; damage from a storm, vandalism or fire; or simply age, wear and tear. This form of depreciation affects both short and long lived items.

Short-lived items are those which have a shorter useful life than the home as a whole. These include the air conditioning and heating system; floor coverings (carpet and vinyl); exterior and interior paint coverings; the roof cover, appliances and other items. These components wear out over time and, due to their short life, must be replaced periodically, before the home as a whole needs to be replaced or renovated.

The typical useful life of short lived items within a home is provided below. Note: life expectancies vary based on quality, use, climate, maintenance, and other factors.

TYPICAL LIFE OF SHORT-LIVED ITEMS

Short-Lived Component	Typical Life in Years
Air Conditioner	10 - 15
Roof Cover	15 - 25
Carpet and Vinyl Floors	7 - 10
Paint	3 - 7
Appliances	10 - 15
Windows and Doors	10 - 20

Long-lived components, on the other hand, are associated with the structural and support systems of a home. These items are not typically replaced unless the home is experiencing a massive renovation or if its systems have become grossly outdated. Long lived items include the foundation, the exterior load bearing walls, the roof support structure, the electrical system, the plumbing system, etc. The typical life of most long-lived components of a home range from 40 to 60 years, depending on type and quality of construction, as well as climate and other factors.

When evaluating a home for physical depreciation, undertake two levels of inspection. The first level is performed by you - the buyer. This is a simple, cursory inspection to rule out any major problems. If the house passes this initial test and you are still interested in buying, then go to the second level - a professional home inspector.

As stated, the first level of inspection is basically a cursory inspection which occurs after your initial walk through of the house. Generally, it involves a second appointment with the sellers and will take and hour or so of time, depending on the size of the home. Both an interior and exterior inspection should be performed. Examine the following items:

Exterior

1. Go around the perimeter and look at all wall surfaces, eaves, soffits, roof lines, and foundation lines. All lines and angles should be straight and true. Bulging walls, sagging roof, and foundation lines, and bowed corners are serious red flags indicating potential structural problems.

2. Open and shut all doors and windows. They should glide smoothly and shut tightly without much effort. If sticking or gaps are present, this may be an indication of settlement or framing problems.

3. If the home is improved with wood siding, eaves, and soffits, or wood window sills and door jams, then poke suspicious looking wet areas with a pencil, pen or other small but sharp object. If the wood is spongy and the point sinks easily into it, then rot is present. If a large portion of the home suffers from rot, then structural damage may be present. However, if only a small area is affected, then it probably is repairable. Sometimes mildew and rot can look alike on the surface. Mildew can be easily cleaned, while rot affects the integrity of the wood. However, prolonged exposure of mildew on wood can lead to rot.

4. Are the roof shingles in good shape, or are they peeling, faded, and stained? If the latter indications are present, then a new roof is probable needed. The cost of replacing roof shingles generally ranges from $1.00 to $2.00 per square foot, depending on type of covering, roof pitch, and area of the country.

Once the outside inspection is complete, then go inside and consider the following:

5. Examine walls and ceilings for watermarks, which appear as dark lines or rings and usually are strong enough to show through paint and wallpaper. Such marks result from flooding, pipe breaks, roof leaks, and other moisture damage. Small isolated areas can generally be repaired, but a contractor should be consulted. If water lines are found in several places, then structural systems may have been damaged.

6. Look carefully at the quality and condition of floor coverings, and ask the age of these components. If floors are worn, stained, broken, or torn, then replacement will be necessary.

7. Look at the paint. Is it new and in good condition, or old, faded, and marked?

8. Check all light fixtures, ceiling fans, exhaust fans and appliances to make sure they are in working condition. Flush all toilets and run water in the sinks, tubs and showers to make sure there are no plumbing problems. Also, check if the hot water is truly "hot" and ask the age of the hot water heater. They generally only last 10 to 15 years.

9. Try out the air conditioning and heating system. Switch on each component and then stand underneath a vent to feel the temperature of the air. Also, check the comfort level in the house. Is it cool inside even though its a hot summer day, or is it warm even though its a cold winter day? A properly operating and sized system should be able to maintain a comfortable temperature and humidity level.

10. If mildew stains are on the ceilings in rooms other than the bathroom, then a moisture problem is present. This means the air conditioning system is not removing excess moisture from the house.

11. Examine HVAC ducts. Are they dusty and dirty, or clean? If the house is old then the ducts will most likely require cleaning; a process which costs in the range of $500 to $1,000.

Lastly, is the house clean and well kept. If a house isn't clean and in good condition when you look at it as a prospective buyer, then think how it usually looks on a day to day basis. A home requires constant maintenance or it will decay. Therefore, an unkept home is generally an indication that proper maintenance has not been performed.

If your initial screening doesn't uncover any significant problems and you are still interested in buying, then go to the next level and hire a building inspector. Such an inspector should be a licensed contractor or appraiser and preferably be a member of a professional home inspection association. For a small fee, generally $200 to $500, an inspector will carefully analyze the condition of a home, identify existing and potential problems, and provide repair costs.

At a minimum, an inspector should examine the structural integrity of the framing; the condition of the exterior siding and roofing; the effects of any settlement, moisture, or insect invasion; the condition of walls, ceilings and floor coverings; and the condition of the electrical, plumbing, and HVAC systems. This includes crawling into the attic and under the foundation (in the case of off-grade construction). Most will provide a brief written report detailing their findings.

When hiring a building inspector make sure he is only an inspector and not also a repairman. Inspectors which also perform repairs compromise their integrity by presenting a potential conflict of interest. In particular, if an inspector examines a home, prepares a detailed report on its condition, estimates the cost to repair noted problems, and also presents an offer to do the repair work, then how are you to know if he has exaggerated problems and overinflated repair costs in the hope of getting the repair work? Therefore, only hire building inspectors which know up front they won't be hired to do any repair work.

Functional Obsolescence

Functional obsolescence is another form of depreciation. It is associated with function, not condition, and pertains to the layout, design and style of a home. There are basically two types of functional obsolescence; deficiencies and superadequacies.

A functional deficiency is present when a home doesn't have the same features of other homes in the area. As a result, it will generally suffer a loss in value. The key to determining functional obsolescence is knowing the features most other homes in an area contain. Some common examples to help you understand the concept of functional obsolescence are presented below:

> Example 1: Assume you are evaluating a home in a subdivision oriented toward young families. The major-

ity of homes have three bedrooms and two bathrooms. The home you are considering has three bedrooms but only one bathroom. Sales in the area indicate that homes with only one bathroom sell for $7,000 less than homes with two bathrooms. They are also more difficult to sell, requiring longer marketing periods. Therefore, the lack of an additional bathroom is a functional deficiency.

Example 2: Assume you are evaluating a home in an older revitalizing section of town. In recent years, most of the older homes have been purchased and subsequently renovated with new electrical wiring, plumbing, central heating, and air conditioning systems. The home you are evaluating has not yet been renovated. It was built in the early 1900s and has original features. Sales indicate non-renovated homes are selling for about $30,000 less than renovated homes. Therefore, the unrenovated home is functionally deficient in the market.

Functional obsolescence can also be due a superadequacy, which is an over-improvement costing more than its resulting value. Examples of superadequacies include the following:

Example 3: Assume you are evaluating a home with an in-ground pool. Sales in the neighborhood indicate homes with pools sell for about $10,000 more than homes lacking pools, all other things being equal. However, the cost to install the pool was $20,000. As such, the cost of the pool is greater than its contributory value, and it is a superadequacy.

Example 4: Assume you are evaluating a home improved with imported Italian marble floors and gold plumbing fixtures. The cost of these features is $30,000 more than the cost of typical finishes. Sales indicate, however, that buyers are only willing to pay $10,000 more for these special features. As such, cost exceeds value and the items are a superadequacy.

The key to understanding superadequacies is to recognize they are not worth what they cost. Therefore, your response to a seller's statement that an item cost "X" dollars to install should be, "So what, it's not worth the cost!"

Just because a home suffers from functional obsolescence does not mean you shouldn't buy it. Just recognize the loss in value associated with the functional problem and don't overpay as a result. For instance, if a home has only one bathroom, you shouldn't pay the same price as a home having two bathrooms. Likewise, if a home has gold plated fixtures, you should only pay the price of a home with typical fixtures.

If a home has a functional problem, then determine if the problem is curable or incurable. A curable problem is one in which the cost to fix the obsolescence is less than the value created, thus making repairs and/or renovations financially feasible to conduct. This can be translated into the following equation:

CURABLE IF:

Cost to Cure < Value Created

The opposite is true of incurable problems, in which the cost to fix the obsolescence is greater than the resulting value. This situation is demonstrated by the following equation:

INCURABLE IF:

Cost to Cure > Value Created

For example, assume a home with only one bathroom is functionally deficient, and recent sales of homes in the area reveal the lack of a bathroom yields a loss in value of $7,000. For this functional deficiency to be curable, the cost to add a bathroom to the home must be less than $7,000. Specifically, if I can hire a contractor and build an additional bathroom onto the house for $5,000, then the deficiency is curable. This concept is demonstrated by the following computations:

Value added by installing an additional bathroom	**$7,000**
Cost to add an additional bathroom	**$5,000**
Difference	**$2,000**

Since the difference is positive, the deficiency is curable.

However, if the cost to add a bathroom equals $8,000, then the following results:

Value added by installing an additional bathroom	**$7,000**
Cost to add an additional bathroom	**$8,000**
Difference	**($1,000)**

Since the difference is negative, the problem is not curable.

Superadequacies are typically incurable. Why spend money to dig up and remove a pool which adds $10,000 in value but cost $20,000 to install? In this case, no extra value is created by removing the pool, so the superadequacy is not curable.

The only time a superadequacy is curable is if the salvage value of the item is greater than the cost to remove it. For instance, assume gold plumbing fixtures and marble floors cost $30,000 to install, but only add $10,000 of value. Further assume that gold and marble prices increase dramatically, and, as a result the salvage value of the marble in the floors and the gold in the plumbing fixtures has increased to $35,000. If the cost to remove these items and replace them with normal fixtures is $12,500, then the superadequacy is curable; i.e., the salvage value of $35,000 is greater than the value loss of removing these items. This concept is demonstrated in the following formula:

Salvage value of items		**$35,000**
Costs:		
Cost to remove items	**$ 2,500**	
Cost to install normal items	**$10,000**	
Loss in value of home as a result	**$10,000**	
Total Cost		**$22,500**
Difference		**$12,500**

In this example, the superadequacy is curable, because the salvage value exceeds the cost to cure. In general, however, superadequacies are rarely curable.

External Obsolescence

The last major form of depreciation is external obsolescence, also known as economic obsolescence. This form is created by a force outside of the property and it is always incurable. Some examples of external obsolescence include a refuse dump being developed next to your subdivision which causes home values to fall; an airport being built nearby with jet landing patterns directly over your house which causes home values to fall; a new highway cutting through your neighborhood; etc.

Probably the most common source of external obsolescence, however, is proximity to railroad tracks. Homes which are built adjacent to or very near railroad tracks experience noise pollution; rumbling and shaking; and the threat of serious injury to children, pets, and other family members and friends. As a result, homes near tracks are often less desirable and suffer a loss in value as compared with similar homes located well away from this type of nuisance.

Most of the time, external obsolescence is beyond our control. However, there are some steps every prudent home buyer should take to try to minimize his/her risks in this regard. These steps were discussed in Chapter 4, *Homesites*, but will be briefly reviewed.

• Avoid living in or near industrial districts. This can be accomplished by thoroughly driving around the neighborhood and looking for sources of pollution and danger such as manufacturing plants, chemical/gas storage facilities, railroad tracks, trucking terminals, airports, refuse dumps, etc. If such are present, look for a house in another neighborhood.

• Examine land use and zoning maps and make sure no vacant areas near the house are zoned for industrial and hazardous uses. Instead, make sure land use maps indicate nearby and adjoining uses will be restricted to houses, parks, schools, and the like.

• Talk to planners, appraisers, and local politicians. Ask what is planned for the area in the future and avoid living near proposed or existing dangerous and obnoxious uses.

Summary

In summary, there are three basic forms of depreciation; physical, functional, and external. Physical is associated with construction materials, functional is associated with design, and external is associated with factors outside of the property directly. The presence of these forms of depreciation result in a loss of value. Home hunters should carefully screen houses for signs of depreciation, and hire a building inspector to perform a thorough analysis before buying.

The presence of depreciation should not necessarily preclude the purchase of a home. However, a potential home buyer should be able to recognize impending problems and not overpay as a result.

8. THE ROLE OF BROKERS

Brokers are market makers. They bring together willing sellers and willing buyers to facilitate a sale. For this service, they receive a fee; generally a percentage of the transaction price. With respect to home sales, the typical brokerage fee ranges from 6% to 7% of the transaction price, or $6,000 to $7,000 on a $100,000 home. This is a large expense, and buyers should carefully weigh the services of a broker versus the cost involved.

Types of Brokers

What are the services of a broker? Well, they may differ depending on the type of broker involved. There are four basic types of brokers, each offering a distinct service within the market. The type is determined by which party the broker represents in the transaction. The four are as follows:

1)   Seller-broker

2)   Buyer-broker

3)   Dual-broker

4)   Transaction-broker

If the broker is representing the seller, then he is a seller-broker. If he is representing the buyer, then he is a buyer-broker. If he is representing both buyer and seller (a very fine line to walk), then he is a dual-broker. If he is representing neither party (just himself), then he is a transaction-broker.

For instance, assume you have been shopping for a home in a particular neighborhood and, one day after driving around, you spot a home for sale which catches your eye. The "For Sale" sign in the front yard includes a local broker's name and phone number, so you call to arrange an appointment for an inspection. The broker then meets you at the appointed time for a tour. The broker also provides information pertaining to the age and square footage of the house, along with type of construction, fixtures to remain, etc. He/She is very friendly and seems to have a commanding knowledge of the area. After completing the guided tour, the broker provides you with a list of other homes in the area that are also being offered for sale. This situation sounds cordial and helpful, but lets examine the implications.

The best indication of who the broker is representing and working for is to discover which party is paying his commission. If the seller is paying the commission, then the broker is working for the seller, not you. While a licensed agent is required by law to be truthful and disclose all relevant information in his knowledge about the home and area, he is not required to look out for the buyer's (your) interest. Quite the contrary, his job is to look out for the seller's interest. He won't get paid until he finds a buyer and consummates a deal. Therefore, carefully examine everything a **selling broker** says and doesn't say. Remember, he is a salesman and you are a prospect.

Another thing to understand about selling brokers is they typically represent many different sellers and products at the same time. For instance, at the end of the home tour in the preceding example, the broker presented a list of other homes he was selling in the area. The broker also works for these sellers. He has a fiduciary contractual relationship with the sellers to protect their interests and sell their homes as best possible, all within a framework of professional honesty and integrity.

The other side of the broker continuum is the **buyer-broker**. This type represents solely buyers. To perform in this capacity the broker must not have any listings; i.e., contracts with sellers to market their homes. The buyer is responsible for paying this type of broker's commission.

For example, assume you are working with a buyer-broker to find the best house and best deal you can in a particular area. The broker identifies a prospect house, but it is listed with a selling broker. The buyer-broker represents you (the buyer) in the transaction, while the seller-broker represents the seller in the transaction. In such cases, the commission is typically split between both brokers by the respective parties.

Beware if a buyer-broker also has listings. Listings are homes the broker is trying to market for sellers. If he is representing sellers while claiming to be a buyer broker, then a conflict of interest is present, for how can he be an advocate representative of a potential buyer and a potential seller at the same time.

This scenario is different than that involving two selling brokers. For example, a potential buyer may go to a broker in search of a house, and the broker may show the prospect a list of homes. However, if the buyer doesn't like any of the listings, then the broker may show the prospect a list of homes listed by other brokers in the area; especially if the broker is a member of a multiple listing service (M.L.S.). If the buyer likes one of the homes listed and decides to buy, then the selling broker (the seller-broker working with the buyer) and the listing broker (the seller-broker which listed the house) split the commission. Recognize that both brokers involved in this typical scenario are seller-brokers, not buyer-brokers.

A buyer-broker works solely for the buyer. They can assist through their knowledge of an area and experience in negotiating deals.

They are fewer in number than seller-brokers, and their services are limited and tailored to a specific clientele. However, if you don't feel confident in doing the market research and deal negotiating on your own, then a buyer-broker can be a good investment. But be fair to them. If you elect to use one, don't milk them for information and then go behind their backs to negotiate a deal on your own.

The next type of broker available in the market place is the **dual agency broker**. This type represents both buyer and seller in a transaction. One minute they may be representing you - the buyer, and the next they are representing the opposing party - the seller. Technically dual-brokers represent both parties. In my opinion, that is a very hard position to maintain. Dual-brokers must disclose their unique type of relationship to both parties and get consenting signatures. My suggestion: stay away from dual brokers. Why pay for no representation?

The last basic type of real estate broker is the **transaction-broker**. He is the antithesis of the dual agency broker. A transaction-broker represents neither the buyer nor the seller; only the transaction. Thus, he is not looking out for the interests of the buyer or the seller; just himself. Yet, both buyer and seller split his commission. Again, why pay for no representation? My suggestion: stay away from transaction-brokers.

You may have to deal with a seller's broker if they have listed the house you are interested in buying. That's OK, because you are not paying their commission. However, beware they do not represent you. If you do decide to use a broker, make sure its a buyer's broker. This is the only type which will represent solely your interests.

Broker Agreements
If you decide to retain the services of a broker, you will have to sign an agreement outlining the service to be provided and the

fee due. For instance, if you decide to hire a buyer's broker, that broker will most likely ask you to sign an agreement covering a specific period of time, generally 3 to 6 months. During this period, you agree to pay him a commission if he shows you a house you later decide to buy. This ensures the broker will be paid for the time and effort spent assisting you.

The broker agreement is fairly simple. It details the parties involved, the time the agreement will be in force, and the services/responsibilities of each. It is important that both parties work in good faith. Typically, a buyer-broker is motivated to work hard on your behalf, for they won't get paid unless you buy something. That means they must show you houses that meet your buying criteria. Therefore, it is in a buyer-broker's interest to find what you are looking for. To assist them in this endeavor, prepare a list of the features and characteristics you are seeking in a home, but recognize that there is no perfect home which will meet all of your criteria. Simply try to do the best you can.

In general, an agreement between a buyer and broker should include the following:

1) The origination date of the agreement

2) The expiration date of the agreement (typically 3 to 6 months)

3) Names and addresses of parties involves; i.e., the buyers and the broker

4) Type of agreement (buyer agency); exclusive or open. (In an exclusive agreement you will only be working with him and not other buyer brokers as well. In contrast, in an open agreement, you can work with other buyer brokers too. Typically, however, buyer brokers will only work under exclusive agreements)

5) The agreed-upon rate of commission/compensation (typically split a 6% to 7% fee with selling broker, but no less
than 3% to 3.5% of the sale price)

6) The type of neighborhood, homesite, and home sought
(general criteria)

7) Signatures of parties involved

Summary

In summary, brokers are market makers who make a living bring-
ing together buyers and sellers. There are four basic types of
real estate brokers; seller-brokers, buyer-brokers, dual agency
brokers, and transaction-brokers. Seller-brokers represent the
opposing party; sellers. Dual agency and transaction-brokers
represent both and neither, respectively. Only a buyer-broker
represents solely the buyer. Thus, I recommend buyers either
shop on their own or with the assistance of a buyer-broker.
However, be aware that in many parts of the country buyer-
brokers are a relatively new thing, and you may only have the
option of dealing with a seller-broker – just keep your eyes open
and ask questions.

Retaining the services of a buyer-broker involves signing an agreement (contract) detailing the responsibilities of the parties involved. This contract is typically for a specified short period of
time (3 to 6 months) and details information such as dates the
contract is in force, parties involved, services to be rendered
and compensation due. The contract must be executed (signed)
by both parties.

9. CLOSING THE DEAL

After researching the marketplace, shopping diligently, and finding the best home option available, its time to close the deal. This is a three step process involving:

1) Negotiating

2) Executing a purchase and sale agreement (contract)

3) Consummating the transaction

These steps are probably the most daunting to home buyers. However, as will be shown, they are relatively easy when you know what to expect.

Negotiating the Deal

The first step toward closing the deal is negotiating. Negotiating is nothing more than communicating in a manner which represents your best interests in a transaction. The good thing about negotiating for the acquisition of a home is the buyer typically has the advantage. This is because, a buyer typically knows the asking price of the seller before negotiations begin. As a result, the buyer knows the seller's upper limit (represented by the asking price), while the seller does not know the buyer's upper limit (represented by how much he is willing to pay). Therefore, the buyer has the upper hand unless he slips up and tells the seller the most he can afford to pay.

Specifically, in the housing marketplace, the list price of homes available for sale are typically advertised in the newspaper, sales brochures, on television, on telephone message systems, and in other media. Therefore, from the beginning, the buyer knows the asking price. As a result, he knows how much the seller will accept and has the opportunity to counter-offer and possibly negotiate a bargain.

This strategy is flipped around on consumers by car salesmen every day. One of the first things they ask shoppers on the car lot is, "How much payment can you afford?" Shoppers relinquish their strength, however, if they reveal this fact, for then the salesman will press a deal to the maximum threshold. In contrast, if shoppers ignore the inquiries of salesmen and press for the best deal available, mentioning nothing of their ability to pay, then they stand a better chance of negotiating a favorable deal.

Lets consider a housing example. Assume I have done my homework and decided to negotiate on a 2,000 square foot house listed for sale. My research reveals other houses in the area have been selling in the price range of $50 to $52 per square foot, indicating a house value of approximately $100,000 to $104,000. Therefore, equipped with this knowledge of values, I have decided to pay up to, but no more than, $104,000. Furthermore, assume an advertisement in the newspaper reports the house is available for sale at an asking price of $95,000. If it is in good condition and not suffering any deferred maintenance requiring repair, then the asking price appears to be at least $5,000 below the value of the house. As such, I stand to gain at least $5,000 of equity by acquiring the house at the asking price.

In contrast, if I did not know the list price was $95,000 and initiated negotiations with an offer of $104,000 (the highest price I was willing to pay), then the seller (if he was smart) would have accepted the $104,000 and laughed all the way to the bank. I would have lost $9,000, which is the difference between the $104,000 I was willing to accept and the $95,000 the seller was willing to accept. Letting the other party initiate the price may result in the other party presenting an offer more favorable than the one I was willing to accept.

While it is important to let the other party go first, it is also important to recognize the initiating party typically begins with an inflated price and will probably settle for something less. For instance, the seller may be asking $100,000 but is perfectly willing to accept $95,000. Recognizing this "seller" cushion should prompt a counter-offer.

Counter-offers should typically be at least 5% to 10% below the asking price of the seller. If the seller outright refuses to accept the counter-offer, and is even insulted at the suggestion, then politely excuse yourself and inform them you plan to continue shopping around. Many times, when sellers see a long awaited prospect walking out the door, they change their minds and either accept the offer or counter with a new proposal of their own.

If the sellers don't budge, but hold fast to their asking price, and you still want to buy the house, then call them later that day and keep counter-offering up to the asking price. This strategy could save you thousands and possibly tens of thousands of dollars. However, don't be greedy. Remember, factors such as location, neighborhood, quality of nearby schools and parks, home style, layout, and construction are more important considerations in buying a house than saving a few thousand dollars on the front end.

When buying a house, the negotiations go beyond just agreeing upon a transaction price. Other factors to be negotiated with the acquisition of a used home (existing home) include whether or not the price includes appliances such as stove/ovens, refrigerators, and dishwashers; mini-blinds, curtains, and other window treatments; ceiling fans; needed repairs, etc.

The Purchase and Sale Agreement

Once a buyer and seller have have completed negotiations, then a purchase and sale agreement can be executed. This type of agreement is a contract between the seller and the buyer with significant legal ramifications. As such, your attorney should review this document prior to signing.

The purchase and sale agreement can either be a standard form with blanks to fill in, or it can be a customized document prepared from scratch. I've used both. The format doesn't matter, just the contents. Requirements vary by state, but most contracts must include specific criteria to be construed as legally valid. At a minimum these include competent parties, mutual assent, legal objective and consideration.

Competent parties means both the buyer and the seller are legally qualified to complete the transaction. It doesn't mean they have to be smart or astute business persons. Typically, competency pertains to legal age and mental state. Specifically, if the seller is an older gentleman who is mentally incompetent due to illness, injury, or handicap, then the agreement would probably not hold up in court if a suit was brought by heirs; even if the seller was the rightful owner of the property. Likewise, if the seller were an orphaned minor, the agreement would probably not be honored. Exceptions would be if a guardian or steward with power of attorney consented to the agreement and also executed the document on the seller's behalf.

Mutual assent refers to both parties being willing participants to the agreement. This means neither are subject to undue duress. For instance, coercion, such as when a buyer tells a seller he must sell at a particular price or face the threat of bodily harm, blackmail, slander, etc., then undue duress is present.

Such an agreement would not be legally binding.

Legal objective and consideration pertain to the purpose of the agreement and type of payment involved. In particular, the law recognizes people don't normally enter into a contract without a purpose or anticipated means of compensation. With respect to a purchase and sale agreement, the objective of the seller is to sell the house and the objective of the buyer is to acquire the same. The consideration involved is the sale price.

A valid contract involves exchange. In exchange for the house, the buyer agrees to pay the seller a designated amount of consideration. Such consideration may involve cash (comprised of buyer cash downpayment and mortgage funds), an even exchange (a house in California for a house in Florida, etc.), or an exchange with boot. An exchange with boot is an uneven exchange involving an item and cash, such as a house in California plus $50,000 for a house in Florida.

The type of deed to be transferred should also be identified in the agreement. A deed is a legal document showing proof of ownership. Deeds come in varieties of form and content, and a competent real estate attorney should be consulted. In general, buyers should seek a warranty deed and avoid a quit claim deed. In a warranty deed, the seller warrants to the buyer that the title being transferred is of good quality and free and clear of all liens and encumbrances. In contrast, a quit claim deed only transfers the seller's rights in the property, not all rights. As such, undisclosed other interests, liens or encumbrances may be present. Therefore, spending a few hundred dollars for a thorough title search and competent legal counsel are wise investments.

The type of title transferred should be the fee simple estate; which is the fullest form of real property interest available, subject only to the governmental powers of taxation, policing, eminent domain (condemnation), and escheat (the right of the government to seize a property if no heirs are present after death). In contrast, fractional interests, leased fee interests, and other forms of less than fee simple estates should viewed with extreme caution.

A purchase and sale agreement should include the following:

1. The seller's name and mailing address.

2. The buyer's name and mailing address.

3. The address and legal description of the property being sold/bought (identification of property).

4. The amount of the purchase price/consideration.

5. The type of consideration (cash, trade, boot).

6. The amount of the earnest money deposit.

7. The amount which will be due at closing (generally the sale price less the earnest money deposit).

8. The date of the agreement.

9. The time frame for performance (typically 90 to 180 days).

10. The type of deed to be transferred (typically warranty deed).

11. The type of interest to be transferred (typically fee simple estate).

12. Signatures of all parties involved.

13. Disclosure of any and all applicable deed restrictions, covenants of title, homeowner association fees, etc..

14. A list of all fixtures and personalty to be included in the sale, such as the refrigerator, stove/oven, mini-blinds, wall paper, water heater, etc. (list everything and don't as sume anything).

15. A clause pertaining to financing. Most contracts include a clause that in the event the buyer cannot qualify for financing within a specified period of time, the contract becomes void and the deposit is forfeited to the seller (be aware of such clauses and pre-qualify with a lender before giving the seller a security deposit).

16. An itemized list of the closing costs to be incurred by each party. These may include, but are not limited to, the following:

• Title insurance policy. This document insures the borrower against potential title defects, such as those arising from liens, undisclosed claims, etc. Before issuing a policy, a title company will research the public and other records in an attempt to discover any pending problems. If the title appears clear and marketable, then the insurance company will insure it, for a fee. This fee is typically paid by the seller, and based on a percentage of the purchase price of the home. Mortgage companies require such insurance before they will lend money for a home acquisition.

Let me give a brief example of how title insurance can be important. I recently appraised a property involved in a title defect legal action. The claimant had bought a riverfront home in an old part of St. Augustine, Florida during the early 1990s, with title insurance. Several years later, the new owners discovered the State of Florida owned a 100 foot right-of-way (ROW) thru their front yard.

This ROW was acquired during the 1940s but not disclosed to the buyers. The title company did not discover the ROW in their research, nor did the seller's reveal it. As a result, the buyer's wanted compensation for the loss in the value and desirability of their property due the presence of the ROW. Fortunately, the title was insured and the buyers had a basis for a suit and the title company was seeking an out-of-court settlement. Had no title insurance been involved, the owners may have had no recourse for compensation and could have suffered great loss.

• Sale commission. If either the buyer or the seller have employed the services of a real estate broker, then the amount due the broker and the party responsible for paying him should be stated.

• Appraisal fee. If a mortgage is being used to assist the buyer in acquiring the house, then an appraisal will generally be necessary. However, all prudent buyers should order an appraisal, whether the mortgage company requires one or not. An appraisal is an important tool which can assist buyer's in making a smart decision. For example, if the appraisal comes in significantly lower than the contract price, then you may be overpaying for the property; potentially losing thousands of dollars. Always word your purchase and sale agreement to state that the appraised value must be greater than or equal to the contract price, or you have the option of voiding the agreement. Buyers are typically responsible for paying appraisal fees.

• Credit report. This expense is typically only associated with mortgage applications/funding, and are therefore the responsibility of the buyer. Such reports typically cost $50 to $75.

• Stamps (taxes) on the deed. Real estate transfers are typically taxed on the state level. The tax rate varies per state, and the seller typically pays this expense. It generally amounts to several thousand dollars.

• Stamps on the note. Mortgages involve the transfer of funds and are usually taxed on the state level. Again, the tax rate varies by state. The buyer typically pays for this expense.

• Survey. If a mortgage is involved, then a survey will be necessary. However, a prudent buyer should order a current survey irrespective of the demands of a mortgage company. A survey shows the property boundary lines and identifies any encroachments, recorded right-of-ways, easements, etc. This information is critical to ensure no buildings, roads, hiking trails, adjoining driveways or other non desirable features are on the property. The seller typically pays the survey expense.

• Termite report. If a mortgage is involved, then a termite inspection report will be necessary. However, a prudent buyer will order such a report irrespective of the demands of a mortgage company. This report should be prepared by a state certified termite inspector to identify any damage or infestation resulting from termites and other pests. This could save you significant dollars and heartache in the long run. Be sure to word the purchase and sale agreement to the effect that if termite or other pest damage is identified, then you have the option of voiding the agreement. The buyer typically pays the termite inspector expense.

• Home inspector report. Many mortgage companies now require a home inspection report for loans used to acquire existing homes. However, a prudent buyer should order such a report irrespective of the demands of a mortgage company. Such a report should be prepared by a state certified contractor and be used to identify any potential problems with the home. The purchase and sale agreement should be worded to include a clause allowing the buyer to void the agreement if any significant problems are identified. In lieu of voiding, however, the buyer may elect to adjust the sale price for the cost of curing any items of deferred maintenance or depreciation discovered.

For example, assume the agreed upon purchase price is $150,000 and the purchase and sale agreement includes a clause relating to a home inspector report. In this clause, the buyer retains the option to void or renegotiate the contract in the event the building inspector identifies any deferred maintenance or problems which will cost more than $100 to cure. Furthermore, assume the building inspector discovers rotten wood in the roof deck and the need to replace the asphalt shingle roof covering. The total cost of repairs is estimated at $3,000. As such, the buyer has the option to either void the contract or negotiate with the seller a reduction in the purchase price to account for the expense of repairing the roof. For minor repairs, a negotiated settlement is probably the best course of action. However, having the option to void the contract is an important recourse for the buyer, especially if major problems are discovered.

• Real estate tax and property insurance expenses. Real estate taxes are typically levied by local government and used to pay for schools, police and fire services. Property insurance protects your investment in case the home is damaged in a fire, storm, or other disaster. The cost of these expenses are typically pro-rated among the buyer and seller based on occupancy during the year.

For example, assume a home has been assessed a $2,400 a year real estate tax expense and you plan to close on July 1. As such, the seller will own the home for six months of the year (January 1 through June 30), and you (the buyer) will own the home for six months of the year (July 1 through December 31). Therefore, the real estate tax burden is pro-rated 50/50, with the seller paying $1,200 (50% of $2,400) and the buyer paying the same. In contrast, if you were closing on October 1, then the buyer would have owned the home for nine months and you will own it for only three months of the tax year. As such, the split would be 75/25, with the seller paying the lion's share of the property tax burden.

There are typically other nominal costs involved, such as recording fees, courier or mailing fees, flood map determination fees, etc. The contract should state that all non-specified fees will be paid by the seller. If the seller won't agree, then word the agreement that these other fees will be split 50/50 in cases where both parties agree the fees are necessary.

If you are building a new home, rather than buying an existing home, then attach a construction addendum to the purchase and sale agreement. In this addendum, include a reduced set of plans and specifications detailing items such as floor plan, elevations, size, exterior colors and coverings, interior features, etc. This will decrease the likelihood of the contractor altering the plans or building something different than ordered. While contractor mistakes and oversights are not common, they nonetheless occur. Having specs and plans attached to the contract protects you from future problems and holds the contractor liable for any mistakes he may otherwise deny.

Before closing on a new home, have a final walk-thru inspection, also known as a punch-out, with the builder. If everything isn't exactly the way it should be, then postpone the closing until the deficiencies are corrected. For example, when my wife and I built a new home, we set an appointment with the builder prior to closing for a final walk-thru inspection. The builder was running slightly late on completing the house, so he scheduled this appointment the day before our closing.

When the day arrived and my wife and I did a thorough inspection, we found several problems, such as the need to touch-up paint, the need to clean tiny paint spills off the carpet, the need to adjust doors and cabinets, etc. We were unhappy with these deficiencies and promptly notified the builder the closing was canceled until all items were corrected. He suggested we close as scheduled and that the items would be corrected later. We refused. Witholding payment was our leverage, so we told him there would be no closing unless all items were fixed. Everything was completed by the time I re-inspected the home the next morning.

The Closing

The closing is the final step in buying a home. It occurs when the purchase and sale agreement brings forth a transaction and a deed (document proving ownership) is transferred from the seller to the buyer in exchange for payment. After the closing, the buyer becomes the new owner of the property. Due to the extensive paperwork and money involved, I recommend a real estate attorney be retained during the closing and present to review all documents and provide advise regarding the mountain of papers you will be asked to sign. Don't skimp here. A few hundred dollars for competent legal counsel is a good investment and can potentially save you significant future losses and heartache.

The closing process can take place anywhere. Typically, however, it occurs in the office of your attorney, closing agent, or real estate broker. During the closing, a ledger type document is followed to account for all items specified in the purchase and sale agreement. This ledger is generally referred to as the settlement statement. Standard forms of settlement statements are available through the U.S. Department of Housing and Urban Development (HUD). Basically, this document includes the following:

Settlement Statement General Information:

- Name and address of buyer/borrower

- Name and address of seller

- Name and address of lender (mortgagee, if applicable)

- Address of property being transferred

- Name of closing agent (if a closing agent is involved; i.e., the name of your attorney)

- Place of closing (i.e., your attorney's office)

- Date of closing/settlement

Settlement Statement Ledger

Following the general information is the ledger portion of the document. The ledger consists of two basic sections. The first is a summary of the basic transaction and the second is an itemized listing of individual costs and responsibilities. The ledger divides these basic sections along a two column format - the buyer's column and the seller's column. The items and cost per each party are then listed and totaled. Specifically, the summary portion (first page) typically includes the following:

SUMMARY SECTION: BUYER'S COLUMN:

Contract sale price

+   Settlement charges to buyer (closing costs)

=   Gross total amount due from buyer

-      Earnest Money Deposit

-      Loan Amount (Mortgage)

-      Other cash or boot

=   Cash due from buyer

SUMMARY SECTION: SELLER'S COLUMN:

Contract sale price

-      Settlement charges to seller (closing costs)

=   Gross amount due seller

-      Earnest money deposit

-      Outstanding mortgage balances (these are the seller's mortgages)

=   Cash due the seller

Note: the seller must pay off all mortgages and liens at the closing to ensure the title being transferred is clear and marketable. Thus, any outstanding mortgage or lien balances are taken out of sale proceeds so the title has no defects. These are seller obligations, not the buyer's .

The Smart Home Buyer's Handbook

The itemized second section of the settlement statement lists all closing costs, allocating them to either the buyer or seller column. These costs include, but are not limited to, the following:

1. Sales commission

2. Loan origination fees

3. Loan discount fees

4. Appraisal fees

5. Credit report fee

6. Pre-paid interest expense

7. Pro-rata share of real estate tax expense

8. Pro-rate share of insurance expense

9. Escrow amounts for future real estate tax and insurance costs for year

10. Title search fees

11. Title insurance fees

12. Attorney fees

13. Recording fees

14. Stamps on deed

15. Stamps on note (if a mortgage is involved)

16. Survey expense

17. Termite inspection expense

18. Home inspector expense

The sum of these closing costs per respective party are then listed under the line settlement charges or closing costs and applied in the summary portion of the statement. Recognize, these closing costs typically amount to several thousand dollars and are not financed with the mortgage. Therefore, in addition to an equity downpayment, buyers must also have enough funds to pay for closing costs. Many times, however, if a new home is involved, the builder will pay all closing costs; incorporating this expense into the price of the home. In this way, the closing costs can effectively be financed with mortgage funds, lowering the amount of cash to be applied in the deal.

The last step in closing the deal is signing all documents, paying the required fees, exchanging funds, and receiving the deed. Now, its time to open a bottle of champagne and celebrate. You have entered the world of home ownership.

Summary
In summary, closing the deal involves three basic steps;

1) Negotiating

2) Executing a purchase and sale agreement

3) Consummating the transaction.

When negotiating a deal, let the other party initiate the process. This is typically a default process in home ownership, for seller's generally advertise their asking price via the newspaper, television, sales brochure or other media. If you are interested in a particular home, then do market research to understand housing values in the area and counter the asking price with an offer of 10% to 15% below your estimate of its market value. Be prepared to counter negotiate up to, but not over, its estimated value. Negotiations also include other items than price, such as which appliances and fixtures are involved in the deal.

Once negotiations are complete, its time to execute a purchase and sale agreement. This agreement is a contract specifying the results of your negotiations and outlining the closing process. The particular costs and responsibilities of the seller and buyer are stated.

Lastly, the closing takes place in the office of your attorney, closing agent, broker, or anywhere. During the closing, the purchase and sale agreement is brought to fruition and a settlement statement is used to account for all funds being transferred. After the closing, the deed is transferred to the name of the buyer.

10. AFTER THE CLOSING – MAKING A HOUSE A HOME

The market research, shopping, negotiating, and buying process is finally over. Now what? Well, there are still a few things to do. On the list are: preparing the house for occupancy, connecting all utilities, moving in the furnishings, establishing a maintenance schedule, funding a reserves for replacement account, and preparing for the inevitable bumps in the road to come.

Preparing the House for Occupancy

Preparing a house for occupancy is a step which varies based on the condition of the home at date of sale. If the home is newly constructed and passed your final inspection prior to closing, then it is most likely ready for occupancy. However, if the home has been previously occupied, then it may need some attention before you and your family take up residence.

It is amazing how different a house can look during a thorough inspection before closing, compared to how it looks once the former owner (or resident) has moved out. A vacant house void of furnishing seems to spotlight every little item of deferred maintenance. For instance, now that the couch, love seat, beds, chairs, and throw rugs are gone, the floor coverings are fully exposed and every imperfection is visible.

There will most likely be matted down areas of carpeting where furniture used to lay, dusty areas not vacuumed for months or years, stains formerly hidden, some nasty scratches in wood flooring, and indentations and stains in the vinyl tile. These are to be expected; the house isn't new. A good cleaning is needed, and now is the perfect time to do it.

If, however, you notice serious tears or large stains in the carpet, cracked tiles, holes in walls, or other major problems not disclosed during your inspection or prior to closing which may have occurred during the move-out, then recourse may be necessary. Such recourse begins by contacting the ex-owners to negotiate a settlement. Therefore, always get a forwarding address.

If the former owners refuse to compensate for damages or undisclosed problems, then you should consult an attorney. In general, the law is in your favor. Yet, recognize it may cost more in legal fees than the cost to cure the damage, so be careful about filing a suit or legal action unless the problem is significant.

While the home is empty, I recommend carpet and wood floors be cleaned. Carpet should be shampooed to the point that it is deep cleaned, yet without soaking the underlying carpet cushion. A wet cushion dries slowly and can become host to a variety of mold, mildew and bacteria. As such, the air conditioner or a de-humidifier should be run for several days at a rate which will remove as much moisture from the inside of the home as possible, thus limiting the potential hazards of dampness being retained in the carpet or padding.

Due these concerns, I recommend a good quality, reputable cleaner be employed. Get three quotes and go with the best company, not the cheapest. The typical fee for cleaning a 2,000 square foot home is a couple hundred dollars.

If the carpet is so bad that a professional cleaning doesn't do much good, then replace it while the house is empty and before you move-in. The cost of removing old carpet and installing new is generally $2 - $3 per square foot.

With respect to wood floors, depending on age and condition, it may be a good time for re-finishing. This generally involves removing the finish coat, sanding the wood surface, and applying a new finish coat. Again, its not as easy as it looks. Inexperience can result in removing too much wood while sanding, resulting in reduced life and a rough, uneven surface. Also, too much finish coat will cloud the look of the wood, while not enough will wear thin quickly. Again, get at least three quotes from experienced craftsmen and go with the best.

While carpet and wood floors should be left to cleaning professionals, the "do-it-yourselfer" can easily clean ceramic and vinyl floors. Ceramic tile is probably the easiest floor covering to clean. The hard surface will not allow dirt build-up, so a good mopping with clean, lightly soapy water generally does the job. Grout is a little harder to clean, however, depending on color and consistency. Grout is the cementuous material which fills in the gaps between tiles, holding them together. A small brush can be used to scrub the grout, and any chips, gaps, or cracks should be repaired.

Vinyl tile is tougher to clean than ceramic tile. Dirt can build-up and get pressed into the vinyl if not carefully maintained over time. Also, vinyl can get dented, torn, stained, etc. Therefore, the condition of the surface will determine whether or not it needs to be replaced. If it is just dirty, then scrubbing with a good brush, mop, and quality vinyl tile cleaner, such as Armstrong brand, will make a dramatic difference.

Once vinyl floors are thoroughly clean, apply a finish coat. The type of finish coat will vary depending on whether it is a "wax" or "no wax" floor. Cleaning is hard, labor intensive work. But, the reward is obvious; a clean and shiny floor.

If the vinyl floors are ten years old or more, or in bad condition, then they should be torn up, the underlying foundation sanded smooth, and a new surface applied. Vinyl flooring is relatively inexpensive and comes in large sheets which are cut and glued to the floor. The cost is typically $3 to $5 per square foot, installed.

It is also a good time for painting while the house is empty. This is something you can do yourself and save several hundred or thousand dollars. Just be sure to use good quality paint and drop cloths to protect the floors. Use rollers on large wall surfaces and brushes on edges and trim. You may also want to consider decorative wall coverings at this time, such as sponge painting, stencil painting, wallpaper, chair rail, crown molding, etc.

Another thing to consider in preparing a house for occupancy is the condition of the heating, ventilation, and air conditioning (HVAC) ductwork. As discussed briefly in a previous chapter, mold, mildew, bacteria, and micro-organisms often begin to grow and live in ductwork over time. As such, ducts should be cleaned if the house is over five years old, especially if a smoker and/or fur or feather bearing animal lived in the house. Duct cleaning involves a high pressure vacuum and sanitizing cleansers to eliminate all contaminants. Special, expensive equipment is required and, therefore, professionals must be hired. The cost is typically $300 to $500 for a 2,000 square foot home.

Get in and scrub clean the bathroom floors, sinks, toilets, counters, cabinets, ceiling fans, and light fixtures. Appliances such as ovens and refrigerators which were bought with the house should also be cleaned. If you don't have the time or energy for such intense cleaning, then hire a maid service. The typical cost is a few hundred dollars.

Its time to buy a lawn mower and get into the habit of lawn

maintenance. Many first time home owners don't think much about lawn care, but it can be an expensive and time consuming task. A push mower will cost a few hundred dollars, a self-propelled mower between $250 and $500, and a rider generally costs in excess of $1,000. Don't forget a weed trimmer ($100), edger ($75 to $200) and blower ($75 to $200) or broom ($10). If you don't want to incur the investment in equipment or time, then there is always the option of hiring a lawn maintenance service. The cost of this service varies based on yard size, foliage, and climate/growing season.

Beware of bug or fungi invasion. A neighbor of mine went on vacation for a week, and when he returned his yard was nearly wiped out by an infestation of worms. It was amazing to see a lush, green yard turn brown and ragged in such a short period of time. Therefore, a well kept lawn will most likely involve the periodic application of pesticides. If you are not comfortable applying chemicals, then hire a service. The cost is generally $25 to $40 per month, but will vary based on yard size, climate, and whether shrubbery care is included, etc.

Connecting Utilities

Shortly before closing on your new house, be sure to establish an account with all pertinent utility companies serving the property. Allow plenty of time, for utility companies often require 3 to 5 working days to establish service.

The type of utilities which need to be connected are a function of what is available. In an urban or suburban setting, electric, water, sewer, phone, natural gas, and cable television are often available. In contrast, a rural setting may be limited to only electric and phone service, with water provided by an on-site well, sewerage disposal provided by an on-site septic tank, and natural gas kept in an on-site tank. Typically, if you are a new customer of the utility provider, then a security deposit will be required along with connection fees. Budget at least a few hundred dollars.

Moving in the Furnishings

Now that you've prepared the house for occupancy and connected all utilities, its time to move-in. Moving is hard work and best left to professionals, especially if you are moving due to a job transfer and your company is willing to pay the cost. This cost varies based on the amount of furnishings and materials to be moved, as well as the distance involved. Typically, at least several thousand dollars are involved. However, if you can afford it, a moving company is well worth the investment. Hiring movers eliminates the risk of hurting your back, popping a hernia, having a heart attack from over exertion, or otherwise damaging your health; which in the long run is much more expensive than the cost of the mover.

If you can't afford a moving company, or if you're just moving across town, then there are alternatives. Since getting married and starting a family, I have moved many times. Each time I moved myself, with the enlisted help of family and friends. I chose this option simply because I couldn't afford the alternative of a moving company, and the distances involved were short.

The financial cost of doing it myself was limited to renting a truck and buying some boxes; amounting to only a few hundred dollars. The physical and emotional cost was much higher. Moving is exhausting. If you decide to move yourself, then U-Haul and Ryder offer a fleet of trucks for rent, with various sizes for various loads. I've used both and was a satisfied customer. With a moving company, they do everything. With a rental truck, you do everything. Some tips for do-it-yourselfers:

• Pace yourself. Moving takes time - several days. Go slow and don't overdue it. Moving is a marathon, not a sprint.

• Enlist as much help as possible. Family, friends and co-workers are the best candidates. Then, treat helpers hospitably, with plenty of food and drink for their time and effort.

• Box and wrap things carefully. The primary reason furnishings get broken, scratched, chipped, or otherwise damaged during a move is because they were not packed properly. Spend a hundred dollars and buy good boxes and packing materials. Wrap dishes, glasses, etc. in newspaper.

• Load the truck properly. Put heavy things in first and on the bottom layer. Then, fill-in and stack up lighter things atop.

• Put extremely fragile items in your car for transport.

• Be sure the truck comes with a dolly and ramp. The simple use of leverage and wheels will save you muscle and back aches.

Establishing a Maintenance Schedule

Its important to promptly establish a maintenance schedule after moving-in. This schedule should include both regular and episodic activities, and be written down and placed in a visible work section of the house. You generally don't need to be reminded that the grass needs cutting, the carpet needs vacuuming, the floors need mopping, the porch needs sweeping, etc. These items are hard not to notice when they haven't been attended to. However, its the episodic items which can slip our minds if not written down.

For example, my maintenance schedule is printed out and attached to a clipboard hanging visibly in the laundry room. On this schedule are the items I must attend to every few months for the house to remain in good condition. After I complete the item per the schedule, I check it off. When all items have been completed for the year, then I make a new schedule for the upcoming year. Episodic items which may be on your maintenance include:

HVAC System: Air filters should be changed monthly or bi-monthly depending on the rate of use of the system and the type of filter employed. Furnaces should be inspected every few years for leaks or other problems prior to the winter season, and fresh batteries installed in smoke detectors and carbon monoxide monitors. Ducts should be cleaned every five years, or sooner if a smoker or pet resides in the house.

Carpets: should be professionally shampooed and cleaned every one to two years depending on use. They should be vacuumed at least once per week.

Wood flooring: should be mopped every one to two weeks, and professionally stripped, sanded and re-finished every five years or so depending on use.

Vinyl flooring: should be mopped with mildly soapy water every one to two weeks, and deep cleaned with Armstrong or equivalent brand cleaner one to two times per year. After deep cleaning, a fresh shine should be applied.

Ceramic tile flooring: should by mopped with clean water every one to two weeks to remove dust and dirt from the surface area. Grout should be cleaned as needed.

Windows: exterior windows should be washed with soap and water one to two times per year, and interior windows cleaned with a good quality window cleaner such as Windex at least quarterly.

Wood and vinyl siding: should be pressure washed to remove dirt and mildew every one to two years depending on climate and air quality in an area.

Doors: hinges should be lubricated with "3 in 1 Oil" or "WD 40" type lubricant one to two times per year, or as needed.

Garage door: hinges should be lubricated with "3 in 1 Oil" or "WD 40" type lubricant one to two times per year, or as needed.

Oven and refrigerator: should be cleaned one to two times per year.

The following page includes a copy of my maintenance schedule. You may want to copy it for your home, or adapt one of your own.

MAINTENANCE SCHEDULE

AIR FILTER: BI-MONTHLY

February _____
April _____
June _____
August _____
October _____
December _____

PRESSURE WASH HOUSE

Spring _____

SHAMPOO CARPETS

Summer _____

OIL DOORS AND HINGES

Spring _____
Fall _____

CLEAN WINDOWS

Outside:
     Spring _____
     Summer _____
     Fall _____

MOPFLOORS:BI-WEEKLY

January _____
January _____
February _____
February _____
March _____
March _____
April _____
April _____
May _____
May _____
June _____
June _____
July _____
July _____
August _____
August _____
September _____
September _____
October _____
October _____
November _____
November _____
December _____
December _____

Reserves for Replacement

Reserves for replacement is a special savings account which should be established to accumulate funds needed to replace short-lived items as they expire over time. As previously discussed in this book, a house consists of long-lived and short-lived items. Short-lived items, unfortunately, don't last very long and must be replaced over time for the house to remain in a good, well maintained condition. Examples of short-lived items include floor coverings (such as carpet and vinyl), roof coverings (such as shingles and shakes), HVAC units (such as heat pumps, air conditioners and furnaces), and appliances, to name a few.

If a reserve fund is not established, then you may not have the money needed to replace the items when the wear out. And, they will wear out, you can bank on that. Therefore, to avoid having to get a loan at a later date or put-off needed replacements, it is wise to establish a reserve fund.

A properly established reserve fund takes into consideration the expected life of the short-lived item, the estimated cost to replace it, and the anticipated "real" rate of return to be realized on the savings account. Note, the "real" rate is used if the replacement costs are current costs, not inflated costs. Remember, a "real" rate is the nominal interest rate less the inflation rate.

Reserve accounts should be established in relatively safe, liquid investment vehicles. Some good ideas are certificates of deposit or professionally managed mutual funds which invest in low risk equities and bonds. High risk ventures should be avoided. The money being invested is intended to protect your home and keep it in good condition, so be cautious. A "real" rate of between 5% and 7% should be achievable.

In estimating the amount to be set aside each month, apply a sinking fund factor. This type of factor is used to calculate the payment needed to accumulate a future sum of money at an indicated interest (yield) rate. The factor is based on the following formula:

$$SFF = I/(((1+I)^{\wedge}n)-1)$$

Where:

SFF = Sinking Fund Factor

I = Interest rate

n = Expected life of item

For example, if an item has an expected life of 15 years and an 8% real rate of return is anticipated, then the sinking fund factor is estimated as follows:

$$SFF = .08/(((1+.08)^{\wedge}15)-1)$$

$$= .08/((1.08)^{\wedge}15)-1)$$

$$= .08/(3.172-1)$$

$$= .08/2.172$$

$$= .037$$

If the item has a replacement cost estimate of $3,000, then the reserve is estimated by applying the sinking fund factor as follows:

Reserves = SFF x Replacement Cost

$$= .037 \times \$3,000$$

$$= \$111 \text{ per year}$$

This same calculation can be applied to all items based on their specific cost and life expectancy. For example, a reserves for replacement schedule associated with a 2,000 square foot brick veneer home may appear as follows:

RESERVES FOR REPLACEMENT SCHEDULE				
Item	Estimated Life (yrs)	Replacement Cost	SFF @ 8%	Annual Reserves
Carpet	10	$3,000	0.069	$207
Vinyl tile	10	$1,000	0.069	$ 69
Shingles	20	$2,000	0.022	$ 44
Ducts Clean	5	$500	0.170	$ 85
Heat Pump	15	$3,000	0.037	$111
Appliances:				
Stove	10	$500	0.069	$ 35
Water Htr	10	$200	0.069	$ 14
Refrig.	10	$700	0.069	$ 48
Total Annual				$613

As can be seen, the total reserves in this case amount to $613 per year, which equates to $51 per month.

Bumps in the Road

Lastly, be prepared for bumps in the road of home ownership. Its not all smooth sailing once the deal is done and you move-in. Little problems tend to arise and typically at the worst possible time, so brace yourself and don't panic.

For example, my family and I recently moved into a brand new house which we had designed and built in a newly developing neighborhood. We moved into the house during September 1996 and, being in Florida, ran the air conditioning for several months to keep cool. Then, in late November, the first cold snap struck, and I went to the thermostat to switch the heat pump from air conditioner mode to heater mode. When I made the switch, the unit went dead.

Initially, I thought a fuse had blown, so I went to the service panel. All fuses appeared in good condition, indicating a more serious problem was at hand. I immediately called the contractor.

Unfortunately, it was late at night when the problem occurred and the contractor reported he couldn't come until the next afternoon. I was forced to spend a cold and uncomfortable night in a brand new house. Fortunately, everything was under warranty and the service call was free of charge. The source of the problem turned out to be an improper connection. After fixing the unit the next day, everything worked fine.

A few months later, another problem arose. The insinkerator (disposal) began making a terrible noise and suddenly stopped working. I crawled under the sink, disconnected the unit and plumbing, and pulled it out for inspection. Just as I suspected, something had fallen inside and jammed the rotor. I dislodged the penny, reconnected the unit and everything worked fine again – but this repair work ate up an entire Saturday morning.

Then, a few months later, more bumps in the road. After coming home from church one Sunday afternoon we discovered the water pressure in the house was extremely low. I called the neighbors, all of which reported their water pressure was normal. This was bad news, so I went outside and walked to the point that the water pipe connects with the house. To my dismay, a small geyser of water was shooting up and flooding the yard. I ran to the garage, grabbed a pair of pliers, went to the street, uncovered the water main connection and shut off all water to the house.

Then, I made a call to our plumbing contractor, who fortunately sent a man right away to repair the leak; which resulted from a pipe disconnection. This also was covered under warranty. Otherwise, an emergency service call on a Sunday afternoon would have cost a small fortune.

As you can see, things go wrong; even with a new house. Parts break and malfunction, often at very inconvenient times. So be prepared for bumps in the road. They are inevitable.

Though problems may occur, you can minimize the impact of these problems with a warranty. Most new homes come with such warranties, but warranties are also available for used homes. The expense of the warranty should be borne by the seller. After all, they should warrant to you the house is in good operating condition. If they refuse to extend a warranty, then a red flag is flying. There may be something seriously wrong with the house they don't want to reveal or insure. Get the warranty in writing, and consult an attorney.

Summary

In summary, work associated with home ownership doesn't stop after the closing, but continues for as long as you own the house. This includes preparing the house for occupancy with a thorough cleaning, connecting all utilities, moving-in, establishing a maintenance schedule and funding a reserves for replacement account. Then there are the unexpected bumps in the road. Try to minimize the impact of such unwelcome problems with a good home warranty paid for by the seller.

11. THE INVESTMENT OUTLOOK FOR HOUSING

You are serious about buying a home as evidenced by your commitment to buy this book and read the preceding ten chapters which provided a detailed look at the housing marketplace. Now, you have a good idea as to what you can afford, what type of house you want, and how you will go about acquiring it. In this last chapter, I want to step back for a moment and ponder the bigger picture. Specifically, buying a house is probably the biggest one-time investment decision you will ever make. Do you know what may happen to your investment dollars?

Many investment advisors tell their clients to buy a house - "You can't go wrong?" Well, you can go wrong; terribly wrong if you're not careful. As with any investment, you can either win or lose depending on the choices you make. There is no guarantee of success. Owners in California and Texas who lost thousands and hundreds of thousands of dollars, watching in horror as their property values plummeted during the recessions of the late 1980s, can attest to the fact that home investment remains a risky venture; even in 20th century America. However, investment risks can be minimized and owners stand a good chance of winning if they are smart buyers.

A home is known as a tangible asset; i.e., an asset you can use and enjoy. All forms of real estate are tangible assets, as are precious metals such as gold and silver and collectibles such as art and antiques. In contrast, intangible assets are typically paper oriented and include stock certificates, bonds, certificates of deposit (CDS), savings accounts, etc.

The difference between the two is a tangible asset can be used and enjoyed while held for investment purposes, while intangible assets lack this consumer use appeal. Therefore, one potential beauty of owning a home is it can be used and enjoyed while hopefully providing investment value.

Owning a home provides the potential for many investment benefits in addition to use and occupancy. The primary investment benefits are capital appreciation, tax shelter/deferral, and leverage.

Capital Appreciation

Capital appreciation occurs when the value of an asset increases over time. For example, if the value of a home increases from $100,000 to $150,000 over ten years, then capital appreciation of $50,000 and an average annual return of 5% ($50,000 ÷ $100,000 ÷10 years = 5% per year) has occurred. This is similar to what happens in the stock market when the value of a share of stock rises from $10.00 per share to $15.00 per share over ten years, yielding capital appreciation of $5.00 per share and 5% per year.

Many factors influence the rate of capital appreciation realized on an investment. With respect to the investment performance of housing, the rate of appreciation is primarily a function of the interaction of supply and demand, and movement in the factors which influence both. For example, as discussed in the life cycle section of Chapter 3 on Neighborhoods, the supply of housing is fairly static (fixed) in the short run period of 3 to 6 months. Therefore, if the neighborhood is in the growth stage with strong demand for housing and if interest rates are low resulting in a good flow of capital to the housing marketplace, then prospects for future appreciation are good. However, if the neighborhood is in the declining stage with soft demand for housing and if interest rate on mortgages are high, then prospects for appreciation are poor indeed.

The Smart Home Buyer's Handbook

The formula used to calculate appreciation is as follows:

Appreciation = Vf - Cost

> **Where:**
> **Vf = Future value of home**
>
> **Cost = Original acquisition cost of home**

And,
> $Vf = Vo (1 + I)^n$

Where:
> **I = rate of appreciation**
>
> **n = holding period**

For example, how much appreciation is expected if a home was purchased for $110,000, will be held for five years, and the expected rate of appreciation is 4% per year. Therefore, the following are given:

Vo = $110,000

n = 5 years

I = 4% per year

Inserting into formula:

Appreciation = Vf - Vo

> $= Vo(1+I)^n - Vo$
>
> $= \$110,000(1.04)^5 - \$110,000$

$$= \$110,000(1.22) - \$110,000$$

$$= \$134,200 - \$110,000$$

$$= \$24,200$$

Tax Deferral, Exemption and Shelter

In addition to providing potential for appreciation, housing investment also provides many tax benefits. One such benefit is capital gain shelter.

Capital gain is a tax term pertaining to the increase in the value of an asset over its original basis (amount paid), after adjustments are made for buying expenses, capital improvements, selling costs, and other items. Capital gains are generally taxable in the year realized; i.e., in the year an asset is sold. Tax laws currently provide varying rates for ordinary gain (salary, commission, tips, etc.) and capital gain (investment gain).

The primary thing to understand about capital gains tax associated with home ownership is a gain of up to $250,000 for an individual and $500,000 for married couples is exempt from taxation. This new treatment of capital gains is a result of The Taxpayer Relief Act of 1997. Former gain rollover requirements and one-time exemptions for people 55 years of age or older no longer apply. The capital gain exemption applies to the sale of a house used as a principal residence for an aggregate of at least two of the preceding five years.

Using the tax exemption opportunities within current tax laws can translate into big tax savings. For instance, consider the following:

• A married couple owns a home free and clear after buying it 30 years ago for $50,000;

- adjustments for buying costs and capital improvements amount to $5,000;

- the current sale price is $150,000;

- selling costs amount to $10,000;

- and the applicable capital gain tax rate is 15%.

The amount of capital gain on the sale of this residence is calculated as follows:

Sale Price of Residence	**$150,000**
- Sale Costs	**$10,000**
= Amount Realized	**$140,000**
- Basis ($50,000 + $5,000)	**$55,000**
= Gain	**$85,000**

Note: the basis is the original acquisition cost plus capital improvements.

Applying a 15% tax rate to the gain of $85,000 amounts to a tax liability of $12,750. However, The Tax Taxpayer Relief Act of 1997 allows $500,000 of gain on the sale of a principal residence to be excluded from taxation. Therefore, no tax liability will accrue to the seller in this case. As can be seen, the use of exemptions can amount to a significant tax savings.

Deductions for Interest on Home Mortgages

The interest associated with a home mortgage is also deductible, except in special situations. This interest deduction is a significant tax shelter. The amount of interest is deducted from the adjusted gross income of the taxpayer in deriving the resulting taxable income. The tax savings (shelter) is equivalent to the tax rate applied to the interest amount.

For example, assume a $100,000 mortgage was used in the acquisition of a $120,000 house, and the annual interest payment associated with the mortgage is $8,000. If the taxpayer falls within the 15% tax bracket, then the tax savings is calculated as follows:

$$\text{Tax savings (shelter)} = \text{Interest} \times \text{tax rate}$$
$$= \$8,000 \times .15$$
$$= \$1,200$$

In other words, as a result of the tax deduction of interest, the taxpayer pays $1,200 less in taxes. This is a big benefit to many homeowners.

Leverage

Leverage occurs when borrowed money is used to help someone with insufficient funds acquire an asset. In other words, if a buyer only has $5,000 to spend and a home costs $100,000, then $95,000 of leverage in the form of a mortgage can be used to acquire the asset. This leverage enables the buyer to purchase something they couldn't on their own; i.e. it helps them reach new heights. However, leverage is a two edged sword and its costs often outweigh its benefits.

The following example explores capital appreciation, leverage and tax shelter.

I live in Jacksonville, a million plus populated metropolitan statistical area (MSA) in Northeast Florida. Jacksonville is an up and coming city which enjoys beautiful sandy beaches along the Atlantic Ocean and miles of scenic wooded frontage along the St. Johns River. It has a mild, Southern climate and a large supply of vacant land available to support future growth and development. In addition, it has a relatively low cost of living (approximately 5% lower than the U.S. average) and is home to a new NFL franchise (the Jaguars), the Professional Golf Association (PGA), the Association of Tennis Professionals (ATP), and the Southeastern branch of the famed Mayo Clinic. In 1997, Money Magazine (April issue) chose Jacksonville as one of the top 10 places to live in the United States.

According to the American Chamber of Commerce Research Association (ACCRA), the average price of a new 1,800 square foot three bedroom two bath home in Jacksonville was $94,713 during the 4th quarter of 1989. ACCRA reports the same type new house sold for $105,523 during the 1st quarter of 1997. Therefore, the capital appreciation associated with the average new three bedroom two bath house in Jacksonville was $10,810 during this reported 7 year period, calculated as follows:

	Vf (1st Quarter 1997)	**$105,523**
-	**Vo (4th Quarter 1989)**	**$ 94,713**
=	**Indicated Capital Appreciation**	**$ 10,810**

The indicated increase in value is $10,810 or $1,544 per year, on average, yielding a rate of return of 1.6% per year. As can be seen, housing values have been appreciating in Jacksonville, albeit slowly.

The return on equity appears better if leverage via a mortgage was involved. For example, assume I had bought the typical

new three bedroom two bath home in 1989 for $94,713 with 5% down and a 95% mortgage, thus using leverage to acquire the asset. As such, I would have invested $4,736 of equity, which is the sale price of $94,713 multiplied by 5%. My loan amount would have been $89,977, which is the $94,713 price multiplied by 95%. If the interest rate associated with the loan was 9.5% and a 30 year monthly payback was involved, then the loan balance at the end of 7 years would have been $84,725. Since the value of the house appreciated to $105,523, then not only would the value of the house increased, but the balance of the mortgage would have decreased through my timely payments. As a result, the equity I would enjoy in the house increased as follows:

		House Value
-		**Loan Balance**
=		**Equity**
Inserting numbers,		
		$105,523
-		**$ 84,725**
=		**$ 20,798**

Therefore, while the capital appreciation of the house overall was $10,810, by applying leverage I increased my equity from $4,736 to $20,798 over seven years; an overall 439% return. In this case, the annual average return on equity was 23.5%. Therefore, the benefits of capital appreciation and leverage are obvious.

The increase in home values, however, must be compared against the increase in the cost of living to determine whether any "real" appreciation was achieved. Remember, "real" means non-inflated.

The consumer price index (CPI), a measure of the cost of living, rose at an average annual rate of 3.6% per year from 1990 through 1996. Therefore, the increase in the cost of living outpaced the increase in the overall value of new homes in Jacksonville over the same period as follows:

Average rate of increase in house value

- **Average rate of increase in CPI**

= **Real rate of return**

Inserting numbers,

    1.6%

- **3.6%**

= **-2%**

As can be seen, in "real" terms, the rate of appreciation is negative. In other words, while my house would have enjoyed 1.6% increase in value, everything else experienced an average 3.6% increase in value. As a result, inflation eroded my increase in value to nothing (in real terms). This demonstrates the danger of inflation.

My equity return, however, is more favorable as follows:

	Average increase in equity
-	**Average increase in CPI**
=	**Real return**
Inserting numbers,	
	25.0%
-	3.6%
=	21.4%

Therefore, the use of leverage has resulted in a quite impressive return on investment, even in real terms.

Unfortunately, the picture becomes bleak when the cost of borrowed money (the cost of leverage) is considered. Specifically, in the preceding example a 95% mortgage ($89,977) at 9.5% for 30 years was analyzed. The cost of this financing includes principal and interest repayment. Borrowed money isn't free. In this case, the monthly payment equates to $756.58.

Therefore, while my equity increased from $4,736 to $20,798 yielding a gain of $16,062, the cost of this gain must be weighted against the cost of leverage, which equates to a payment of $756.58 per month over 7 years, or $63,553. As can be seen, the equity increase of $16,062 is dwarfed by the cost of leverage financing of $63,553. The net cash to cash gain is a negative $47,491 as follows on the next page:

Increase in Equity		**$16,062**
Cost of Leverage (borrowed money) -		**$63,553**
Cash on Cash Return	=	**($47,491)**

As can be seen, leverage is a two edged sword. While it allows me to buy something I couldn't afford on my own and increases the performance of my equity, its huge cost offsets all of my investment returns. This always occurs when the rate of capital appreciation is less than the cost of financing as indicated by the loan interest rate. Specifically, in this example, the rate of house appreciation (overall) was 1.6% per year while the cost of debt capital was 9.5% per year. Since the cost of debt exceeds the rate of appreciation, the leverage is negative.

What if the tax shelter benefits of investment are factored into the analysis. As previously reported, tax laws allow the interest paid on a home mortgage to be deducted. In the example provided, the payment on the typical three bedroom home was $756.58 per month. Over 7 years this payment equates to $63,553, of which $58,301 is interest and $5,252 represents a reduction in principle. Assuming the average middle income tax bracket of 15% is applied, then the tax savings equates to $8,745 over 7 years, which is calculated at 15% multiplied by the interest cost of $58,301. Adding this tax savings to the equity increase of $16,062 yields the following:

	Increase in equity	**$16,062**
+	**Tax savings (shelter)**	**$ 8,745**
=	**Total**	**$24,807**

This total is still woefully short of the cost of debt capital of $63,553. There are no significant capital gain issues in this case. The following summarizes the investment return of the home example discussed.

COSTS:

Downpayment	$4,736
Payments on mortgage for 7 years (P & I)	$63,553
Total Costs	$68,289

BENEFITS:

Equity build-up over 7 years	$20,798
Tax Benefit (interest deduction)	$8,745
Total Benefits	$29,543

RESULTING INVESTMENT PERFORMANCE

	Benefits	$29,543
-	Costs	$68,289
=	Profit	($38,746)

In this example, an investor would have spent $68,289 to gain $29,543. It doesn't take a rocket scientist to realize this isn't a very smart investment.

How does this information reconcile with the stories we've been told of amassing huge amounts of wealth through home ownership? Well, lets examine the basis of these stories. Most come from people who bought their homes back in the 1960s and 1970s and owned them for a long period of time. These homeowners rode the big wave of housing appreciation which occurred during the 1970s and 1980s. The past rates of appreciation are a result of several factors, but the two most significant are 1) the maturing of the baby boom generation and 2) periods of high inflation.

First, the baby boomers. In the 1940s and 1950s, just after World War II, there was a rapid increase in the number of babies being born. Sociologists termed this post war generation the "baby boomers." Twenty-five and thirty years later (during the 1970s and 1980s), the boomers began to mature into adults and started entering the housing market. Home prices soared due to the surge in demand created by the large number of persons seeking housing.

Unfortunately for the housing market, baby boomers didn't have as many kids as their parents, and the birth rate fell dramatically during the 1970s and 1980s. Sociologists termed this new generation the "baby busters." These busters are currently in their twenties, some in their early thirties, and are entering the housing market. However, there are proportionately fewer busters than boomers. As a result, there is proportionately less demand for housing than in the past and rates of appreciation have slowed dramatically.

Inflation is another factor which contributed to past rates of housing appreciation. The table below provides U.S. inflation rates per year from 1960 thru 1996.

U.S. INFLATION RATES PER YEAR (1960-1996)

Year	Annual Inflation	Year	Annual Inflation
1960	1.7%	1980	13.5%
1961	1.0%	1981	10.3%
1962	1.0%	1982	6.2%
1963	1.3%	1983	3.2%
1964	1.3%	1984	4.3%
1965	1.6%	1985	3.6%
1966	2.9%	1986	1.9%
1967	3.1%	1987	3.6%
1968	4.2%	1988	4.1%
1969	5.5%	1989	4.8%
1970	5.7%	1990	5.4%
1971	4.4%	1991	4.2%
1972	3.2%	1992	3.0%
1973	6.2%	1993	3.0%
1974	11.0%	1994	3.6%
1975	9.1%	1995	2.5%
1976	5.8%	1996	3.3%
1977	6.5%		
1978	7.6%		
1979	11.3%		

The graph below illustrates these inflationary trends.

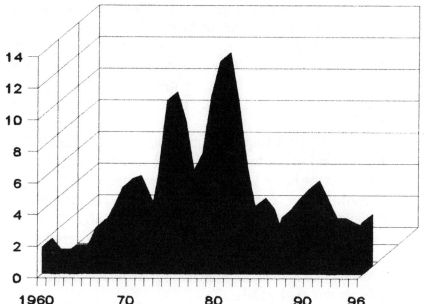

As can be seen, inflation was low in the first half of the 1960s, as it had been in the 1950s. Then, during the Vietnam War, inflation began to edge upward. In the 1970s and early 1980s, inflation shot up into double digit numbers. Runaway inflation was tamed during the Reagan and Bush administrations, and currently, under the Clinton administration, inflation is hovering in the 2% to 4% range. Very low indeed. Most economists are predicting inflation to remain low in the short term future.

Inflation affects the real estate market in several ways. If demand and supply are in relative balance, then home values will typically increase during periods of inflation. This is logical since inflation is a measure of the increase in the cost of goods and services. If the cost to build a home increases because of inflation, then people have to spend more money to buy it. The people which already own their homes then benefit from this upward influence on values.

Inflation was highest during the 1970s and early 1980s, and this corresponds with the period in which most people enjoyed a large increase in the value of their homes. Therefore, its true that many people saw the value of their homes increase dramatically during the past twenty years. However, the benefit they realized is relative, for as the value of their home rose, so did the value and cost of other homes.

For example, lets assume a couple bought a home in 1970 for $40,000, and sold it twenty four years later for $140,000. The couple sold the home because they were retiring and wanted to move into a new condominium. Their home was paid off and they sold it themselves, so they pocketed $140,000 in cash. However, after shopping prices, they soon discover alternate housing costs were at least $100,000, if not more. Therefore, while the price of their home increased, so did the price of other homes in the marketplace.

The above example is commonplace, and many people have sold their houses only to realize later the only way to take advantage of big equity returns are to move into an area with a lower cost of living where they can buy more home for less money, or downsize into a smaller, less expensive home. Therefore, as a result of low inflation and lower proportionate demand created by the baby bust generation, real increases in home values have been relatively slow in recent years. Barring another war or oil crisis, most economists are projecting this trend to continue in the short term future.

A recent article published in the April 1997 edition of Money magazine predicts the top 10 housing markets in 1997 will be San Francisco, Portland, Seattle, San Jose, Salt Lake City, Minneapolis/St. Paul, Miami, Orlando, Houston, and Denver. The current median price and projected value appreciation during 1997 of a home in these cities, and the country as a whole, per the article is provided as follows:

MEDIAN PRICE AND PROJECTED VALUE APPRECIATION

City	Median Price	Forecasted Appreciation
San Francisco	$280,900	5.5%
Portland	$146,600	5.2%
Seattle	$172,600	4.9%
San Jose	$279,000	4.9%
Salt Lake City	$131,300	4.9%
Minneapolis/St. Paul	$123,800	4.7%
Miami	$118,400	4.2%
Orlando	$ 97,000	4.2%
Houston	$ 87,300	4.2%
Denver	$138,600	4.2%
United States	$ 87,400	3.1%

As can be seen, even the Nation's best rates of appreciation are forecasted at 5.5%, and the country as a whole is expected to experience appreciation of only 3.1%. At the same time, inflation is projected to range from 2.5% to 3.5%. Therefore, the U.S. median home price is forecasted to struggle to keep pace with inflation, and the best housing markets will perform only slightly better. From this data, it should be apparent that, at least for now, buying a home should not be looked upon as a fantastic investment, especially if borrowed money is involved.

Recognizing these trends, what rate of appreciation must occur to earn a positive return on a house investment over five years if borrowed money is involved. Specifically, assume a house was acquired for $125,000 using a 90% loan-to-value mortgage resulting in a mortgage loan of $112,500 and an equity downpayment of $12,500. Furthermore, assume the interest rate on the mortgage loan is 8% and the amortization (payback) period is 30 years in monthly installments, resulting in a monthly principal and interest payment of $825.50. The cost of real estate taxes and insurance is $200 per month, which when added to the monthly loan payment yields a total housing cost, excluding utilities and maintenance, of $1,025.50. What rate of appreciation must occur over five years to earn a positive return on investment?

The inputs are summarized below:

Cost = $125,000

Equity = $12,500

Mortgage loan = $112,500

Interest rate = 8%

Amortization period = 30 years, monthly

Real estate taxes and insurance costs = $200 per month

Total monthly housing cost (excluding utilities and maintenance) = $1,025.50

Investment Holding Period = 5 Years

The first step is to estimate the total cost of owning the home (not including utilities or maintenance) over a five year period. This cost equates to the equity downpayment of $12,500 plus five years of payments at $1,025.50 per month, equating to a total cost of $74,030.

Therefore, to earn a positive return, the house must appreciate in five years to a future value of $181,000 in order to break even, resulting in a return of investment but no return on investment. This rate of appreciation equates to an overall increase of 45%, or 9% per year. As can be seen, this rate is far in excess of the forecasted appreciation rates reported. Therefore, at least in the short run, investment in a house does not appear to offer a promising rate of return.

Even though housing shows dismal investment prospects in the near term future, I still recommend buying a house. The reason: though I seldom recommend anyone buy a house to make money, I often recommend people buy a house if it is the place they want to live and raise a family.

Forget about money. Think about quality of life. Think about things more important than investment return such as quality of schools, neighborhoods, proximity to work and health care, comfort, playgrounds, libraries, friends and family. These are the things which make a house a home, not financial return. In general, housing is an expense, not an investment.

Summary
In summary, a house is a tangible asset which can be used and enjoyed while, hopefully, increasing in value over time. The primary investment benefits associated with home investment include the potential for capital appreciation, tax benefits associated with interest deductions and capital gains deferral/exemption, and the use of leverage.

Leverage involves the use of borrowed funds and allows many buyers to acquire a home they otherwise could not afford. However, leverage is a two edged sword, and the lender generally wins at the expense of the borrower. Specifically, the cost of debt financing typically eats up most home investment returns.

Most economists and real estate analysts are forecasting low inflation and interest rates in the short term future. As a result, the expected rate of return on a house is generally not much better than the return available on a safe, savings account. Therefore, carefully consider the investment prospects of housing before you buy. My advice, forget about making money on a house and buy only if its the place you want to live and raise a family. Most of the time, housing is an expense, not an investment.

12. STRATEGIES FOR SUCCESS

The information on the investment outlook for housing presented in the preceding chapter was somewhat sobering. Therefore, in this chapter I want to present some words of optimism. There are ways you can beat the odds and win in the housing market if you are smart and do your homework. In particular, there are five simple strategies which should help limit your investment losses and possibly allow you to even make money.
These strategies include:

1) Buying below market value

2) Creating value

3) Piggybacking

4) Buying in off-peak seasons

5) Avoiding the impulse buy

Strategy #1: Buying Below Market Value
The first of the five strategies is to buy or build a home below its market value. We've all heard the investment advice to buy low and sell high, especially in reference to the stock market. Well, this advice also applies to housing. To maximize performance you should seek to buy a home below its market value, and later, at date of disposition, seek to sell it above market value.

This way you create equity "going into the deal" and you won't be so reliant on future rates of appreciation. This is important since short term appreciation is forecasted to be minimal as previously discussed.

Buying a home below value means you must first obtain a good feel for values. This is not as difficult a task as it appears. The best way to achieve this result is hire an appraiser as a consultant. It may cost $50 to $100, but will be money well spent. Ask for a list of recent home sales near the house you want to buy. Take the list and go look at the houses which have recently sold. Then, compare these sales to the house you want to buy and ask the appraiser if he concurs with your findings. With this method, you will gain valuable market knowledge.

Building a home below its market value involves the same analysis. Basically, just compare the cost of building the new home (including the cost of acquiring the homesite) to the resale value of other homes in the neighborhood. A proposed home is financially feasible from an investment standpoint if the cost of development is less than or equal to the sale value of other homes nearby. This concept is reflected in the following equation:

$$Vo > Po$$

Where: **Vo = Value of Proposed Home**

Po = Price of Other Homes in Neighborhood

For example, assume you are interested in building a three bedroom two bath ranch style home containing 1,800 square feet. The home will have brick veneer and be located on an interior lot. Furthermore, assume the following sales in the neighborhood have been identified:

The Smart Home Buyer's Handbook

Sale	Bed/Baths	Age	Sq. Ft.	Veneer	Lot	Type	Price
1	3/2	3	1,900	Stucco		Corner	$120,000
2	3/2	4	1,700	Wood		Interior	$100,000
3	3/2	3	1,800	Brick		Interior	$110,000

Based on these sales, it appears the best comparable is Sale No. 3, for it shares the size, veneer and lot orientation. Therefore, the value of the house you are interested in building should be worth at least $110,000 and probably more since it is new.

Once you have performed an appraisal (either by yourself or via a professional), begin negotiating with sellers by offering less than the value of the house, regardless of the asking price. Then, during negotiations, be prepared to concede your offer up to market value, but no higher. In this way, you buy the home you want, yet attempt to get the best deal possible.

When applying this strategy, keep the following points of caution in mind:

- Don't search for deals. Instead, search for the home you want, then work out a deal. Otherwise, you may get a great deal, but realize shortly thereafter you don't really like the house. Get your priorities straight.

- Don't take advantage of people in desperate circumstances. Only buy a home if both parties benefit from the deal. The guilt you will feel from taking advantage of someone in a desperate situation is not worth any advantage gained in your equity position. For example, if the seller is facing severe financial problems as a result of a business failure or catastrophic illness, or if the seller is a recent widow or widower, then pay market value or look elsewhere. I know this sounds crazy to the ruthless money minded investor, but I believe in the golden rule; do unto others as you would have them do unto you. In the long run you will reap higher returns.

• There are several instances you may come across where the seller is motivated to accept a below market price to facilitate a deal, yet is not under duress. Such cases include when the seller is moving to another town to accept a promotion or has built a new house and is seeking to sell their old one before moving. These are not dire straights, but chosen opportunities of sellers. Use your conscience as a guide.

Strategy #2: Create Value

To minimize losses and maximize equity potential you should seek to create value by purchasing a home in need of additions or repairs. This is also known as the "home improvement" or "fix-r-upper" strategy. The key point to remember in undertaking this venture is the cost of renovation must be less than the value created.

For example, my wife and I got a bargain on a house once because it was in need of cosmetic work and finishing touches. Specifically, it needed landscaping, shutters, wallpaper, interior and exterior painting, and other such make overs. Therefore, after buying the home, we seeded the yard, redirected the driveway, planted shrubs and flowers, painted the inside and out, and put up wallpaper, chairail, and shutters.

These were relatively inexpensive additions, but the visual effect and increased market appeal was tremendous. Such finishing touches can make one house more valuable than another and help it sell quicker too. The value created by such renovations is often termed "sweat equity" when the owner does the labor himself. We sold the house six years later for a handsome profit, and this was during the real estate depression of the early 1990s.

The Smart Home Buyer's Handbook

Let's examine another example. Assume you are evaluating a run-down "fixer-r-upper" in an otherwise well maintained middle class neighborhood. The home is similar in size and style as other homes in the area, but needs painting, landscape work, and new carpeting. Most homes nearby which are in good condition with nice yards, landscaping and new or fairly new carpet have been selling for $90,000 to $95,000.

You call a contractor and he gives you an estimate of $10,000 to paint the house, sod the yard, plant shrubbery and flowers, and replace the carpeting. Deducting this cost to cure these items ($10,000) from the value of a home in good condition ($90,000 to $95,000) yields the highest price ($80,000 to $85,000) you can afford to pay. If you pay more, then the work will not create any value. You can make even more money if you do the work yourself and save on labor costs.

In general, when evaluating additions or renovations to a home, don't bite off more than you can chew. If the house needs electrical work, hire an electrician; if it needs plumbing work, hire a plumber; if it needs structural changes, hire a carpenter, etc. Be sure the workers are licensed and insured, and get an estimate in writing before you begin. In this manner you will know costs and values before committing to the deal. I have seen too many people buy old homes in a popular revitalizing part of town and then spend far more than its resulting value on costly renovations. This is fine if the home is what you want, but don't expect to get your money back.

Lastly, repairing and renovating a home is a literal pain. Don't undertake such an endeavor unless you can afford the time, inconvenience, sore muscles and cost. My wife and I spent nearly every weekend over the course of several years putting the finishing touches on our home. We were willing to do this, and even enjoyed it. However, we were young, adventurous, and didn't have children at the time. Now, we're not so young or adventurous, and our children and busy schedules consume all our time. As such, it would be difficult to undertake a similar venture today.

Strategy #3: Piggyback

To minimize your losses and maximize equity potential attempt a "piggyback." If you get a piggyback ride, then you are hoisted onto someone else's shoulders, enabling you to reach new heights. Similarly, if you buy in a community where other people's homes are more valuable and expensive than yours, then you can piggyback to higher values. There are two primary ways to achieve this result; through location and home type.

Let me use my experience again as an example. One house we bought was located on a large estate sized lot (1.7 acres) in a lakefront community on the outskirts of town. Most of the lakefront homes were selling within the range of $150,000 to $250,000, while non-lakefront homes were selling at lower prices, generally in the range of $90,000 to $150,000. The closer the location to the water, the higher the value of the house. The house we bought was located across the street from the lake. Therefore, we piggybacked off the high value of the waterfront properties across the street.

A similar principle applies in regard to size. Lets assume you are evaluating a home in a subdivision which is deed restricted and the minimum allowable home size is 2,000 square feet. Based on your research, the vast majority of homes in the subdivision are being built in the range of 2,500 to 3,000 square feet, which is far in excess of the minimum requirements. You can piggyback off the higher value of these large homes by building at the minimum size of 2,000 square feet. Thus, the larger homes will pull up the value of your smaller home (if the majority of homes are larger), all other things being equal (i.e. construction, features, architecture, etc.).

Strategy #4: Buy During the Off-Peak Season

In basic economics, price is the point where the supply curve meets the demand curve. In the short run (i.e., less than 6 months), the supply of homes in a market is relatively fixed. However, demand is elastic, often changing with the seasons. Demand for housing is usually highest during the spring and summer months as families seek to secure a home before the new school year begins in the fall, and because people tend to be more outdoors oriented and explorative during these months.

Since demand is highest at this time, resulting prices are also highest. In contrast, demand is typically lowest during the fall and winter months. In particular, most families don't want to move once school begins and they don't like to move during the holiday months of November and December, when time is devoted to family matters. Therefore, in periods of low demand, prices are softest and deals can be made. If possible, try to buy a home during off-peak seasons.

Strategy #5: Avoid Impulse Buying

To minimize losses and maximize equity potential is to avoid impulse buying. Never sign a contract without first going home to talk with your spouse, pray earnestly, and sleep on it. Then, wait at least 24 hours and consult your attorney. If things still feel right and it is the home you want, then sign the contract in peace. Take it slow. You're better off taking your time and blowing the deal, than rushing matters and regretting it later.

One last word in this regard. Builders, brokers, bankers, and government officials have labored hard to make the home buying process easier and more accessible to all Americans. In general, they have been successful in this endeavor and have contributed to many people realizing this part of the American Dream; which is good. However, potential home buyers should recognize these parties also earn their living by building, selling, financing and taxing real estate. You are their source of revenue. A builder doesn't make money unless he sells a house.

Therefore, weigh carefully his assurance of a well built and suitable product? Likewise, a real estate broker doesn't make money unless he closes a deal, so don't be swayed by his advice and assurances? And, since the compensation and job security of most bankers is based on the number of loans they close, don't be duped by their friendly willingness to lend you money, lots of money? Realize who you are dealing with. As they say, let the "buyer beware."

Summary

In summary, there are five strategies which can help minimize losses and maximize your equity return on a home investment. These include buying below market value, creating value, piggybacking, buying during off-peak seasons, and avoiding impulse buys. These strategies are easy to understand and every home buyer can apply them if interested.

ADDENDA: SUMMARY CHECKLIST

The following checklist can be used when evaluating homes in your area. It summarizes the major points discussed in the text. Please recognize that there is no perfect home and it is highly unlikely you will ever find one that meets all of your criteria. However, by using this list, you can optimize your choice and identify the best housing option available in your particular marketplace.

How Much Can You Afford
Types of mortgages:

    FHA   ____

    VA   ____

    Conventional   ____

    Unconventional   ____

Interest Rates

    Fixed   ____

    Variable (Adjustable Rate - ARM)   ____

Points (Pre-paid interest; avoid)   ____

Origination fees (avoid)   ____

Payback (amortization) period

    Function of stage of life and financial ability

    15 years   ____

    20 years   ____

    30 years   ____

Sources of mortgage funds:
    Banks   ____
    Credit Unions   ____
    Life insurance companies   ____
    Mortgage brokers   ____
Housing Expense Ratio (HER)   ____
Total Obligations Ratio (TOR)   ____
Real Estate Taxes   ____
Property Hazard Insurance   ____
Cash available for downpayment   ____
Qualified loan amount   ____

Location

Roadway Linkages:
    Fronts a secondary feeder street   ____
        Two Lane   ____
        Lightly Traveled   ____
        Not a Thru-Street   ____
    Doesn't front a primary traffic arterial   ____
    Near a primary traffic arterial   ____
    Near a limited access highway   ____
    Near Mass Transit Station (if available)   ____

	Miles	Travel Time
Destinations		
Place of Employment	___	___
School	___	___
Parks	___	___
Shopping Centers:		
Neighborhood/Grocery	___	___
Community/Discount Store	___	___
Regional Mall	___	___

Medical Care:
    Doctors:
            Family physician   ___   ___
            Pediatrician   ___   ___
            OB/GYN   ___   ___
            Dentist   ___   ___
            Optometrist   ___   ___
            Other specialists needed   ___   ___
    Hospital emergency room   ___   ___
    Primary care center   ___   ___
    Fire/Rescue station   ___   ___
Away from nuisances:
    Landfill/Dump   ___   ___
    Industrial Facilities   ___   ___
    Power Plants   ___   ___
    Airport   ___   ___
    Railroad Tracks   ___   ___

Neighborhoods

Economic Cycle:
    Growth (safest)   ___
    Maturity (mostly stable)   ___
    Decline (avoid)   ___
    Revitalization (risky, but upside)   ___
Percentage of Owner Occupancy   ___
Population in 1980   ___
Current Population   ___
Is Population Growing?   ___
Median Age   ___
Median Income   ___
Neighborhood Boundaries:
    Natural; i.e., lakes, rivers, mountains, etc.   ___
    Man-made; i.e., roads, bridges, dams, etc.   ___
Planned Capital Improvements
    Roads   ___
    Schools   ___

Parks ___
Water/Sewer Plants ___
Fire stations ___
Police stations ___
Tax burden:
Property tax rate ___
Sales tax rate ___
Income tax rate ___

Homesites
Type:
Urban
Suburban ___
Rural ___
Part of Platted Subdivision (lot) ___
Size:
Square feet ___
Acres ___
Large Lot = Privacy
Small Lot = Social Interaction ___
Shape:
Square ___
Rectangle ___
Triangle/Pie
Irregular (avoid) ___
Orientation:
Corner ___
Interior ___
North/South (optimal) ___
East/West (energy expensive) ___
Elevation above that of surrounding property? ___
(see topo map)
Any wetlands? (see wetland inventory map) ___
Grade:
Gently sloping away from home placement ___
(optimal)

Radical slope   ____

Flat   ____

FEMA Flood Map Location:

Outside 500 Year Flood Plain   ____

Within 100 Year Flood Plain   ____

Access:

Asphalt paved   ____

Concrete paved   ____

Dirt or Limerock   ____

Tree lined   ____

Street lights   ____

Curved to slow traffic   ____

Publicly Owned and Maintained   ____

Privately Owned and Maintained   ____

Sidewalks   ____

View:

Typical   ____

Waterfront   ____

Quality of water   ____

Other; such as mountain view   ____

Utilities:

Public Water   ____

Public Sewer   ____

Well   ____

Septic Tank   ____

Telephone   ____

Electricity   ____

Gas (lines or on-ste tank)   ____

Cable television   ____

Residential Zoning   ____

Land Use Plan   ____

Deed Restrictions   ____

Homeowner's Association:

Annual fees   ____

Liability insurance policy   ____

Organizational make-up   ___
Reserves for replacement   ___
Architectural review   ___
Legal Description:
    Lot and block   ___
    Metes and bounds   ___
    Government survey   ___

Design
House Type:
    Attached (share at least one common wall) ___
    Detached   ___
Distinct Zone Placement
    Social   ___
    Private   ___
    Work   ___
Single or multi-story   ___
Access Point at Each Zone   ___
Ceiling height   ___
Orientation:
    North/South (optimal energy efficiency)   ___
    East/West (poor energy efficiency)   ___
Side or Front Entry Garage (side preferred)   ___
Friendly Front (concrete walk, porch, and foyer)   ___
Minimal Hallway Space   ___
Kitchen triangle concept   ___

Construction
Mark trees to save with fluorescent   ___
tape and drip line barriers
Foundation:
    On-Grade   ___
    Off-Grade   ___
Exterior Wall Framing:
    Masonry   ___
    Wood   ___

Steel   ___

Exterior Wall Veneer:
 Concrete Block   ___
 Brick   ___
 Stone   ___
 Coquina   ___
 Stucco   ___
 Wood Siding   ___
 Wood Shakes   ___
 Plywood   ___

Roof type:
 Gable   ___
 Hip   ___
 Gambrel   ___
 Flat   ___
 Shed   ___
 Other   ___

Roof Cover:
 Shingles   ___
 Shakes   ___
 Ceramic Tile   ___
 Metal   ___

Exterior Doors: (Not Hollow)
 Solid Wood   ___
 Metal   ___
 Combination   ___

Interior Wall Framing:
 Wood Studs   ___
 Metal Studs   ___

Interior Doors:
 Hollow Core   ___
 Solid in Master Bedroom and Study   ___

Wall Coverings:
 Paint   ___
 Wallpaper   ___
 Paneling   ___

Stenciling ____
Crown molding ____
Chair rail ____
Floor Coverings:
Carpet and padding ____
Vinyl Tile ____
Ceramic Tile ____
Wood ____
Electrical System:
Two Prong ____
Three Prong (best, most modern) ____
HVAC System:
Central ____
Room ____
Heating Fuel:
Electric ____
Combustible Gas ____
Combustible Oil ____
Lighting:
Fluorescent in kitchen ____
Incandescent or fluorescent in bathrooms ____
Spot fixtures ____
Ceiling fan kits ____
Security System
Entry ____
Motion ____
Advanced ____
Home Office System
Separate fax and Internet line ____
Built-in desk and cabinetry ____
Quiet part of house ____
Landscaping
Yard cover ____
Shrubbery (keep trimmed low for security) ____
Function of climate and soils ____
Irrigation system ____

Evaluating an Existing Home

Physical Depreciation:

Age of House	___
Sagging Roof Line	___
Cracks in Walls or Foundation	___
Bulging Walls	___
Rotten Wood	___
Water Marks on Walls or Ceiling	___
Windows Open and Shut Easily	___
Doors Open and Shut Easily	___
Condition of Paint	___
House is Clean and Well Kept	___
Air Conditioning is Cold	___
Heat is Hot	___
Hot Water is Hot	___
Faucets don't Leak	___
Toilets don't Run	___
No Dirt/Dust Marks at HVAC Vents	___
Roof Shingles Peeling/Cracking	___
Carpet Stained or Torn	___
Carpet Loose or Wrinkled	___
Vinyl stained or Torn	___
Ceramic Tile Chipped or Broken	___
Are Repairs/Renovations Curable?	___

Functional Obsolescence

Deficiencies	___
Sometimes curable	___
Superadequacies	___

External Obsolescence: (avoid nuisances)

Railroad tracks	___
Garbage dumps	___
Industrial facilities	___
Major highways	___
Airports or military bases	___

The Role of Brokers
Types: Who do they represent?
  Buyer-broker ___
  Seller-broker ___
  Dual-broker ___
  Transaction-broker ___
Types of agreements:
  Exclusive (work only with them) ___
  Non-exclusive or open
  (can work with others also) ___
Agreement should specify:
  Time period involved
  (no more than 3 to 6 months) ___
  Service involved ___
  Commission rate involved ___
  Parties involved ___

Closing the Deal
Negotiating:
  Know the asking price ___
  Know values of homes in the area ___
  Counter offer below the asking price,
  then up to, but not above the asking price ___
Purchase and sale agreement:
  Seller name and address ___
  Buyer name and address ___
  Description of property ___
  Price/consideration ___
  Ernest deposit ___
  Date ___
  Time for performance ___
  Type deed to be transferred
  (Warranty Deed) ___
  Type interest to be transferred
  (Fee Simple) ___
  Personal property and fixtures involved ___

Itemized list of closing costs
and who will pay for them:
    Title insurance (typically seller)   ___
    Commission (depends on type
    broker involved)   ___
    Appraisal (typically buyer)   ___
    Credit report (typically buyer)   ___
    Stamps (taxes) on deed
    (typically seller)   ___
    Stamps (taxes) on note
    (typically buyer)   ___
    Survey (typically buyer)   ___
    Termite report (typically buyer)   ___
    Warranty (typically seller)   ___
    Home inspector report
     (typically buyer)   ___
    Real estate taxes (pro-rated)   ___
    Property insurance (pro-rated)   ___
    Recording fees   ___
    Attorney fees   ___
    Other fees   ___
Closing:
    Generally in office of attorney or broker
    Settlement statement:
        Calculations of cash due from buyer___
        Calculation of cash due to seller,
        less outstanding mortgages and liens___
        Listing of closing costs
        and party responsibilities   ___

After the Closing – Making a House a Home
Preparing for occupancy (before you move-in):
    Have carpets professionally
    cleaned or replaced   ___
    Have wood floors refinished   ___
    Clean or replace vinyl flooring   ___

Clean or repair ceramic tile flooring   ____

Clean bathrooms   ____

Clean kitchen and appliances   ____

Paint (if needed)   ____

Clean HVAC duct work (if needed)   ____

Buy yard maintenance equipment:

     Mower   ____

     Trimmer   ____

     Edger   ____

     Blower   ____

     Other   ____

Connect utilities:

     Electricity   ____

     Water   ____

     Sewer   ____

     Gas   ____

     Cable   ____

     Phone   ____

     Other   ____

Moving:

     Use professionals if possible   ____

     For do-it-yourselfers: rent a truck and dolly   ____

     Pace yourself   ____

     Get lots of help   ____

     Box and wrap carefully   ____

     Put very fragile items in car   ____

Maintenance schedule:

     Air filters   ____

     Batteries in smoke and CO detectors   ____

     Carpets and floors   ____

     Windows   ____

     Hinges   ____

     Appliances   ____

Reserves for replacement:

     In safe, liquid account   ____

For:

Roof   ___

HVAC system   ___

Floor coverings   ___

Paint   ___

Appliances   ___

Other   ___

Be prepared for bumps in the road!

Strategies for Successful Buying

Buy below market value   ___

Search for your dream home, not a dream deal   ___

Don't take advantage of people
in desperate circumstances   ___

Create value   ___

Piggyback off the high value of others   ___

Buy during the off-peak season   ___

Avoid impulse buying (sleep over all decisions)   ___

INDEX

The Smart Home Buyer's Handbook

The Smart Home Buyer's Handbook

OPEN ROAD PUBLISHING

Open Road publishes travel guides to more than 60 great destinations. We now also publish running and home handbooks. We welcome your input, so please send your comments and suggestions to:

The Smart Home Buyer's Handbook
Open Road Publishing
PO Box 284
Cold Spring Harbor, NY 11724